THE
FEMININE
UNCONVENTIONAL

OVERTURES TO BIBLICAL THEOLOGY

Editors

*Four
Subversive
Figures
in Israel's
Tradition*

THE
FEMININE
UNCONVENTIONAL

ANDRÉ LACOCQUE

FORTRESS PRESS   Minneapolis

THE FEMININE UNCONVENTIONAL
Four Subversive Figures in Israel's Tradition

Scripture quotations are translated directly from the original languages by the author.

Library of Congress Cataloging-in-Publication Data

Lacocque, André.
    The feminine unconventional : four subversive figures in Israel's tradition / André Lacocque.
        p.   cm. — (Overtures to biblical theology)
    Includes bibliographical references.
    ISBN 0-8006-1559-X (alk. paper)
    1. Women in the Bible. 2. Bible and feminism. 3. Sex role-
-Biblical teaching. 4. Bible. O.T.—Criticism, interpretation,
etc. I. Title. II. Series.
BS1199.W7L33   1990
221.9'22'082—dc20   89-48026
                                                              CIP

The paper used in this publication meets the minimum requirements of American National Standard for Information Sciences—Permanence of Paper for Printed Library Materials, ANSI Z329.48-1984.   ∞™

Manufactured in the U.S.A.   AF 1-1559

94   93   92   91   90   1   2   3   4   5   6   7   8   9   10

To Clyde and Ardis Manschreck
Their commitment is a reflection
of the fortitude displayed by
the characters in this book

Contents

Editor's Foreword

In his treatment of Judith, the second of four commentaries on stories "that speak about women," André LaCocque reflects on the paradox that Judith—more "woman-oriented" than (the conceivably female-authored) Susanna—was probably written by a man. He concludes that while paradoxical, the situation deserves to be celebrated: "The best advocates for a cause are those who are not self-serving." With just a slight wink to the reader, La-Cocque appears to plead his own cause here, as in *The Feminine Unconventional* he celebrates the underrepresented but bold interventions of women on behalf of God, for Israel and the world. Susanna, Judith, Esther, and Ruth are individual examples of the triumph of four "subversive" figures in Israel's history. Together, as a literary genre, they represent the persuasive and masterful way stories can make their truth known. In LaCocque's able hands, one sees the potential for change not only in the bold or cunning actions of four *figurae,* but also in the power of narrative art and imagination.

A man writing on women in the Bible does not itself make an Overture to Biblical Theology, less still an overture to the politics of biblical studies or an overture to biblical anthropology. This is true even as LaCocque advances several theses, some more controversial than others, about the role of men and women in the Bible. In chapter 2, for example, he argues that maleness and femaleness in Israel have more to do with psychological and social realities than anything we might designate simple "biological" marking. These realities demand balance and mutuality

ix

between the sexes, and point to identity discovered and brought to fulfillment in relationship with the other. So, LaCocque speaks of "... the genders as contingent instead of absolute, as relational instead of self-contained." Failure to respect this fact does not go without consequence in Israel. The feminine is "unconventional" in these four women's stories in order that the proper relationship between the sexes might be restored, at a period in Israel's history when the constitutive role of women is most threatened. We discover that a theological reality and purpose is also at stake.

The historical and lexical support for LaCocque's thesis is set forth in the opening two chapters. With reference to the work of Norman Gottwald and Carol Meyers, LaCocque argues that in the premonarchic period greater attention was paid to the appropriate balance between the sexes. Though departures from this ideal could be detected in the preexilic period, the most severe rupture is seen to exist in postexilic Israel, in "the edicts of Jewish governors dissolving marriages." Susanna, Judith, Esther, and Ruth, it is argued, represent a form of protest literature aimed at correcting the situation.

Elements of this thesis will certainly be challenged. Reading Ruth against Ezra-Nehemiah has a venerable history. But the power of the proposal lies in an area unrelated to historical reconstruction as such. LaCocque gives himself the occasion to comment on these four stories—two of them extracanonical—*as a group,* and to detect within them certain consistent features. He brings to this task a clear and often brilliant literary analysis, uncluttered and straightforward. As a result, four underread books are introduced and set in perspective before our eyes, their individual characteristics not subsumed under a master theory nor left scattered and unrelated. In this sense, the thesis does not drive the commentary with a heavy hand. Rather, it enables LaCocque to make some valuable observations about biblical anthropology through the lens of four masterfully constructed stories.

The final effect is an overture as much literary as anthropological. Within both realms, LaCocque detects a unifying vision, focused on what he identifies as *peripeteia,* or the sudden turn of fortune. Both through the actions of these four women and through the narrative art of the stories themselves, a "change of fortune" is brought about. As a consequence, this "subversive literature" strikes a welcome balance with the broader literature of the Hebrew Scriptures. At the same time, a theological overture is made: women are acknowledged for the concrete and indispensable role they play in Israel's salvation history. Without them, God's will cannot be done; the salvation history cannot move forward, nor can it save. As literature and as individuals, Susanna, Judith, Esther, and Ruth accomplish a *peripeteia* that allows God to convict, convert, and save.

Christopher R. Seitz
Yale Divinity School

Preface

The "Four Subversive Figures in Israel's Tradition"—as the subtitle of this book reads—include in succession Susanna, the central character of an Addition to the book of Daniel in Greek; Judith, the heroine of an Apocryphon to the Old Testament; and two of the biblical feminine figures, Esther and Ruth. The present book adopts naturally an obvious pattern with essays on these figures constituting the core chapters. These are framed by an introduction to the status of women in the ancient Near East, and more particularly Israel, and a conclusion reflecting upon the motif that ties together this medley of traditional texts dating from different periods, although all belong to what can be called the Second Commonwealth subversive literature in Israel. Hence the title *The Feminine Unconventional.*

These essays are, in more elaborate and readable form, lectures I was invited to deliver at Rice University, Houston, Texas, in March 1987, in the framework of the Rockwell Lectures. They originally included in their title the word "Figurae," taken in its initial meaning of models or types (before it became imitations or copies).[1] Thus was the term "heroines" avoided—because of its ambiguity, due to a large extent in the West to the ancient Greek ideal of heroism, which has made such an impact upon our way of thinking,[2] while the Hebrew world leaves so little room for

1. See E. Auerbach, "Figura," in *Scenes from the Drama of European Literature,* 11–76.
2. It has, for instance, made inroads in Carl Jung's vocabulary about the conquest of the unconscious. On the discovery of heroism's failure to provide

such display of "machismo" valor. But while that unwelcome aspect was thus left aside, it was from the outset made clear that the feminine figures under consideration are presented in the Hebrew tradition as *models* to follow, not as strange phenomena deserving mention only because of their weirdness. The latter conclusion was not unambiguously foreclosed. All four figures, though some more than others, are indeed unconventional. They stand out from the ordinary. They all display aspects of notoriousness that can make one wonder about their setting examples to be emulated. One is accused of fornication; another uses wiles and ostensible wantonness; a third shares the bed and table of a pagan "male chauvinist"; and the fourth not only comes from a loathed nation that had made itself noteworthy by procuring its own females as prostitutes to seduce the Israelites before attacking them, but she seems to repeat that kind of misbehavior herself on a since-famous threshing floor!

Clearly, the nation's leaders, in charge of making far-reaching decisions as to the trustworthiness and authority of some traditional texts, versus other documents that would be set aside as "external books," as they were to be called, had to weigh those aspects—which their general conservative stance would put in the debit column—over against other elements, such as the punctilious piety of Judith and the moving fidelity of Ruth. That they agreed to include two of the documents in the canon and to exclude the other two leaves us with an uneasy feeling of awe and disappointment, like someone thirsty before a half-full—and half-empty—glass of water.

I want to thank Rice University Department of Religious Studies for the opportunity afforded me to work on these fascinating documents. They have been a source of great joy, and I hope that the present book will convey some of it to my readers. I am gratified to know that among the latter are the good friends to whom I dedicate it.

immortality, see J. M. Redfield, *Nature and Culture in the Iliad: The Tragedy of Hector.*

Abbreviations

AB	Anchor Bible
APOT	R. H. Charles, ed., *Apocrypha and Pseudepigrapha of the Old Testament*
ATD	Das Alte Testament Deutsch
B.B.	*Baba Bathra*
BDB	F. Brown, S. R. Driver, C. Briggs, *A Hebrew and English Lexicon of the Old Testament*
BTB	*Biblical Theology Bulletin*
CAT	Commentaire de l'Ancien Testament
CBQ	*Catholic Biblical Quarterly*
Diod. Sic.	Diodorus Siculus [= of Sicily]
E	Elohist [or] Esther literary source
Ency. Jud.	*Encyclopedia Judaica*
HAT	Handbuch zum Alten Testament
ICC	International Critical Commentary
IDB	*Interpreter's Dictionary of the Bible*
J	Yahwist
JAAR	*Journal of the American Academy of Religion*
JBL	*Journal of Biblical Literature*
JJGL	*Jahrbuch für jüdische Geschichte und Literatur*
JQR	*Jewish Quarterly Review*
JSOT	*Journal for the Study of the Old Testament*
JTS	*Journal of Theological Studies*
K-B	L. Koehler, W. Baumgartner, eds., *Lexicon in Veteris Testamenti Libros*
m.	Mishna

M	Mordecai literary source
MGWJ	*Monatsschrift für Geschichte und Wissenschaft des Judentums*
P	Priestly literary source
P.K.	*Pesiqta Kahana*
Pesiq. R.	*Pesiqta Rabbati*
R.	*Rabba*
RB	*Revue Biblique*
RHA	*Revue Hittite et Asianique*
RHR	*Revue d'Histoire des Religions*
RLA	*Reallexikon der Assyriologie*
Sanh.	*Sanhedrin*
Shabb.	*Shabbat*
Test.	Testament
Tg.	Targum
Tos.	*Tosephta*
TZ	*Theologische Zeitschrift*
Vg.	Vulgate
VT	*Vetus Testamentum*
WZKM	*Wiener Zeitschrift für die Kunde des Morgenlandes*
Yad.	*Yadayim*
Yebam.	*Yebamot*
Z.	*Zuta*
ZAW	*Zeitschrift für die Alttestamentliche Wissenschaft*

CHAPTER 1

Introduction

There are four documents from the ancient Jewish tradition—both biblical and extrabiblical—that share two striking characteristics. First, and most obviously, they speak of heroines, a somewhat surprising phenomenon in Jewish literature, which is usually preoccupied with male heroes. Second, these four documents belong, as we shall see, to a literature of protest that arose at a specific period of Israel's history in response to particular circumstances. Thus we shall deal with the "feminine unconventional"—or, more specifically, with four examples of subversive literature of the Second Temple period in which the central figures are women.

As far as I can see, the situation of women in Israelite society was exacerbated during the time of Ezra-Nehemiah, the fifth century B.C.E. This is not to say that all was smooth and nonproblematic with regard to the relationship between the genders in preexilic Israel. But the Jewish governors in Jerusalem, appointed by Persian rulers, demanded that Jewish men divorce the foreign wives that many had married, either before their return to Zion or after they settled there.[1] This, as we can imagine, made a strong impact on Jewish consciousness. According to our sources, the new laws were generally obeyed, but not without significant resistance and opposition. Nehemiah 6 speaks of a prophetess by the name of Noadiah, who, "with the rest of the

---

1. In Babylon, contacts with other ethnic groups were of course frequent. Among the returnees to Zion, males outnumbered females and thus looked beyond the pale for wives.

prophets," opposed the governor. If Nehemiah nonetheless succeeded, it was only up to a point. Numerous were particular cases when the protest became more and more articulate. It eventuated in a literature that, due to the circumstances, had to express its subversive opinion in cautious forms. One of the favorite vehicles chosen for that purpose was popular stories or tales putting heroines on the center stage. More pointedly, these women were presented as Jewish (like Susanna) or non-Jewish (as in the case of Ruth); as rising to social eminence by their personal qualities (like Esther) or through highly questionable means (like Judith)—or even a mixture of the two. The four heroines under consideration here are cases in point: Ruth allures Boaz by invading the privacy of his "bedroom," Esther is wife to a pagan king, Susanna is accused of fornication and adultery, and Judith plays harlot with Holofernes. The intent of such stories is clear. They want to drive home the idea that women can indeed become God's instruments, even when they use the most controversial resources of their femininity. Consequently, to assign them to a lower status of citizenship in the community or, worse, to treat them as disposable goods, would be a grave mistake as well as a grave injustice.

The measures taken in Jerusalem by Ezra and Nehemiah occurred among diverse attempts of the returnees to restore conditions that had prevailed before the exile in Babylon. A real effort was made during the Second Temple period to restore a pristine conception of sacred Israel, before it had been damaged or eventually destroyed by what the prophets denounced as the people's sinfulness. The dream of some was to put in brackets the Babylonian catastrophe and to link the present times with the old age by jumping over the exilic hiatus. As the deportation had been caused by sin and impurity, and itself constituted a sinful and defiled situation, it was felt necessary to make people recover their purity through their rejecting all ties with the secular and the profane, that is, with the "world."

The protest literature shared with the conservative party a similar striving for sanctity, considered to be an indispensable condition for the advent of the much-anticipated restoration. But its program was vastly different, and its model went further back in time beyond David or the erection of the Temple, indeed to the very origins of Israel. It is immaterial whether or not the image that the literature had of Israel's origins was accurate. As the Israelite tradition—particularly the prophetic—has it, the beginning was most beautiful; it was the time of betrothal between God and the People. In more than one way this was the ideal to retrieve, the epoch of *verus Israel* (genuine Israel) that should never have been lost.

One of the fronts where the protest literature chose to build up pressure was the issue of women. In doing so, it was reviving an ancient idea of liberty and equality that was constitutive of the community's consciousness at its inception. This was not baseless. Modern sociological studies show that Israel as a people was born with the proclamation of a revolutionary ideal that clashed with a Canaanite conception of sacral kingship and authoritarian despotism. Israel seems to have been the outcome of a movement of liberation that proclaimed freedom for farmers and shepherds who were determined no longer to comply with tyrannical and dictatorial sanctions of the city-kings in the region. Such a revolution requires an intentional egalitarianism at all levels of the society.

The early egalitarianism, however, soon had to compromise the ideal by an equitable division of labor and responsibility that would protect weaker members of society, particularly physically disadvantaged persons and mothers with infants. This need not be interpreted as a purely altruistic move; it was a correct application of the instinct of survival.[2] It was, however, almost inevitable that what was originally meant to be a protective measure for some, especially women, became a means of inferiorization first on the level of economic worth, and then in terms of ethical and ontological value. Although that situation was never really systematized and justified by subsequent traditions, it became a de facto condition of Israelite women.

As we have seen, this situation exploded, so to speak, with the return from exile. The occasion was provided by the edicts of

2. See Carol Meyers, *Discovering Eve,* especially chapter 3 "Setting the Scene: The Highland Environment of Ancient Israel," 47ff. On survival, see for instance 56.

Jewish governors dissolving mixed marriages. This was tanta-mount to the idea that the problematic element in Israelite soci-ety was women and that the nation's spiritual health demanded the expulsion of those among them who could not prove their Jewishness. It is the first time in biblical history that "Jewish-ness" becomes a quality to be preserved from foreign contamina-tion.[3] Earlier, to be sure, there had been "foreigners," and these were collectively called "the Nations." But the shift to Jewishness as an ontological quality endangered by the non-Jew is a new development. Before Ezra and Nehemiah, the danger came from the religious beliefs and practices of "heathens." The aliens were not as such unwelcome in Israel; they even were invited to partic-ipate in the festivals and other religious-cultural activities with the Israelites (cf. Lev. 16:29; 17:8; 22:18, among other passages). Intermarriages must have been numerous and not scandalous, as the relatively late composition of the patriarchal stories, for example, proves. The transformation by Ezra and Nehemiah of the Jewish nation into a sect, however, shifted the character of Jewish identity as it switched the sequential order covenant–commandment into commandment–covenant. In other words, from fundamentally unconditional, the alliance with God be-came the outcome of Israel's purity, even ethnic purity. Between Hosea and the Chronicler there is a long way.

With a sure instinct, the Second Temple scribes quickly fo-cused on the generative process in the community. Before they could define Jewishness as a birthright *and* an achievement, they had first to drive home the paradigm of election-selection. The people elected are the people selected, who, in their turn, proceed constantly to select not only their commensals and "concele-

---

3. This was due to the fact that Persia granted to the exiles a status based on religion. The Temple and its clergy became preeminent and the Torah the state law of the Jews. A similar situation obtained, for instance, in Egypt, where the so-called demotic chronicle shows that Persia codified the local laws and promoted them to the rank of state law. The result was a definition of nationality by religion, with the consequence that the national identity itself felt threatened by the presence of foreign elements. They could not be tolerated, at least in the views of Ezra and Nehemiah. In the fifth century, therefore, there began that Jewish exclusivism so much criticized by the Greeks and Romans in the following centuries. On all this, see E. J. Bicker-man, *The Jews in the Greek Age*, especially chapter 6.

brates" but also their connubials, as the three Jewish characteristics had now become *kasheruth* (dietary laws), Sabbath keeping, and circumcision.[4]

Table, family celebration, bed—in all of these three major aspects of Jewish life, women play a crucial role. Even when that role is seen as ancillary, it is clear that a great deal of the sanctity of the occasion rests in women's hands. Ezra and Nehemiah were true reformers; they chastened the feminine, like Paul of Tarsus or John Calvin would do, because they realized that it is the root of societal identity. By the time of the Persian-appointed governors, the inequality between the sexes was in any case so deeply rooted and considered so "natural," that many in Israel did not really question the gubernatorial authoritarian decision. It had indeed become customary, in some milieus, to regard the feminine as morally devious, if only because of its perceived capacity for outward display of weakness and helplessness used as an artful, transparent veil over its immensely powerful sex appeal.[5]

Be that as it may, when, against the Chronicler's conception,[6] protest arose, its literary production necessarily went "underground" in order to survive the censure of the authorities. The fact that two of the four documents that I propose to review are extrabiblical points in the same direction. When, around the year 100 c.e., the Rabbis proceeded to decide which books or parts thereof would be canonized (recognized as authoritative), they tended to regard the subversive literature of the Second Temple period as nonbinding in matters of faith and practice.[7] Susanna and Judith fell victims of that ostracism. As is well known, the Rabbis' canon of Scriptures was by and large accepted by the early Christian church. Whether it is legitimate for us to bring

4. Incidentally, the term *ger*, stranger, was later reinterpreted to mean "convert."

5. Judith comes to mind. The book might have been written by a woman, for all we know, but the story is clearly told from the male point of view!

6. I consider the Chronicler's work as including the books of Ezra, Nehemiah, and Chronicles *(pace* H. G. M. Williamson, *Ezra and Nehemiah).*

7. I adopt here for simplicity's sake the traditional view on how the canon came into existence at the Rabbinic academy of Yavneh towards the close of the first century c.e. The truth of the matter is more complex and the canonization process more protracted. Yavneh is a relay station on the route to the Scripture canon.

together for the sake of study that which the canonizers have put asunder is therefore an issue that must be dealt with from the outset.

Can we put Judith and Susanna on a par with Ruth and Esther without disrespect for the canonical status of the latter two? The question is complex, and any response to it has serious consequences. It would take us beyond the limits of this study to deal with it in some fullness. But the general situation produced by the canonization of selected traditions and the rejection of others allows us to draw several conclusions. In the canon there are documents that escaped censure because they contain redeeming details. Ruth was received because of the Davidic genealogy of chapter 4 that makes her an ancestress of the anointed king. The apocalypse of Daniel was accepted because of the demonstrations of the piety of the man (chaps. 1–6) and of his power of interpretation and prediction (chaps. 7–12). The Esther scroll was the legend of a public celebration, the festival of Purim. Conversely, there are documents that were refused entry into the canon because of their known date of composition or because they contain elements that the Rabbis censured. Among the so-called Additions to Daniel, for example, some qualify in this latter category, especially Susanna despite its intrinsic "orthodoxy." The same can be said of Judith. In brief, the periphery of the canon is a shaded area rather than a firm borderline. To be critical of the canon is a matter of respect for the canon. It is a service rendered to the canon to prevent its foreclosure. The area around the canon is shaded for different reasons—from sheer unworthiness on the plane of value to strong divergence on the level of doctrine. In the latter case, the critiquing of established authority is a most important instrument in the constraint of official religion.

CHAPTER 2

The Status of Women
in the Ancient Near East
and in Israel

THE WOMEN IN THE ANCIENT NEAR EAST

Societies in the ancient Near East, at least since the beginning of the historical period, were of the patriarchal type, that is, they were based on patrilinear succession. Characteristic in those societies was the lower status of woman. She was "in the care," first of her father or elder brother, then of her husband. The prevalence of the patriarchal type of society both in time and in space has socioeconomic roots. For obvious reasons, the most representative kind of marriage, in that region of the world as well, is the exogamous one. Its origins go back to the dawn of hominization. It was dictated by the need for alliances between humans involved in communal activities such as big-game hunting. In dangerous endeavors such as this, mutual trust is fundamental. As brothers-in-law are natural partners with powerful blood-ties, they fulfill this need.

Communal survival depends upon the delicate balance between human integration within nature and resistance to nature. Going out to hunt or to wage war, symbolically at least, is a sign of such loosening from the coils of nature; women remain the stable element, to which there is the rhythmic return after the military or hunting campaigns. At those very moments begins culture, for culture consists, first, of the symbolization of the acts of valor out there "in the field," then, second, of the symbolization of the familiar and the customary. All of these transcend their immediate usefulness because they repeat the archetypes of *illud tempus* (that mythical time). They are meaningful, noble, poetic, religious. The universe and the human share a common language. The world has a voice and the human is its mouthpiece. The symbol brings them together. "The symbol makes one think" (P. Ricoeur). Through reflection, the human transcends his or her limits and overcomes death—or, at the very least, insignificance.

Symbolization entails typologization. A man hunting becomes *the* hunter; a woman nursing becomes *the* mother. All exemplars must display a capacity of mirroring a consciousness deeply rooted in a given category: all men must be able to recognize themselves in *the* hunter, and all women in *the* mother. The process of identification goes so far as to become reversible. At some point, roles are distributed according to the representation of the symbols. Rather than symbols fitting the privileged acts, acts shift to the level of roles, and roles fit the symbols. A woman *is* a mothering human being; a man *is* a hunter.

Eventually, the symbol makes one not only think, but also reach out to the stars, so to speak. It makes one worship. For the role symbolized is ultimately attributed to the divine. The masculine role is hunting or warring, because the god is the Hunter and the Warrior par excellence. Hunting and warring are not only symbolic representations; they express the essence of the god. Men hunting and warring are not only duplicating divine activities; they are acting the divine act, they are raised to a divine level, pulled to another world more real and more beautiful than the secular world. As the symbolized feminine role represents the stability of the natural cycles—a stability more hoped for than actually experienced—it is not surprising to see the cosmos as a whole represented by the Mother Goddess, or the Great Mother, or again the Mother Earth, to whose embrace one hopes to return after death, thus completing the cycle of life. This symbolism is powerful; it shows in a definitive way that the human may go afield and trace a more or less vast circle of life experiences, but that there inevitably is a return to the womb, an eternal return. In the beginning is the mother; at the end is the mother.

Of particular importance for us is the fact that, from a socioeconomic as well as from a symbolic religious point of view, the female principle was assigned its moorings in the cosmic, the earthly, the natural and also, as we shall see, in the refinement of intelligence, understanding, and harmony, the capacity of soothing anxiety over death. Consequently it took courage and determination for the male to tear himself from the female solace and go outside to the hostile world and confront the animate and inanimate forces. As Miguel de Unamuno wrote, "The will and the intelligence seek opposite ends: that we may absorb the world in ourselves, appropriate it to ourselves, is the aim of the will; that we may be absorbed into the world, that of intelligence...."[1]

Such a statement must be taken with some flexibility. It is all too tempting to exaggerate its bearing and pit intelligence and will against one another in a dualistic fashion. It is, however, somewhat striking that the most "intelligent" culture in the world, Greek civilization, emphasizing as it did timeless reason, set as the highest goal for individual and society *harmonia* (which can be translated, "law," "order"). Harmony, says Will Durant, "was literally worshipped by the people as a god."[2] On the other hand, a culture like the Hebraic, which invests so much in the willful "making of the truth," undertakes to "subdue the earth" (see Gen. 1:26-29).

This is not the place to react against the facile opposition between Athens and Jerusalem. But we must once again emphasize that the contrast between will and intelligence is a matter of balance and proportion. What is stated here is simply this: it takes intelligence rather than will to live in harmony with the world, and it takes will rather than intelligence to shape the world or reality to fit one's dreams or ideals. Conceiving and giving birth contribute to the cyclical looping of the cosmos, and in that respect are intelligent acts of survival, intelligent celebrations of life. But creating in realms other than organic is an adventurous and risky endeavor that has its roots in the precosmic, *in illo tempore* (in that time before time) of the myth. Sumerians already associated brick-making and building with the creation of the world. They were followed in this by all Mesopotamian peo-

---

1. Miguel de Unamuno, *The Tragic Sense of Life,* 113.
2. Will Durant, *The Story of Civilization,* 2:575.

ples. Around 2000 B.C.E., the Babylonian version of the Sumerian myth "Enki and the Ordering of the World" shows that the organization of the world by Enki is a great construction of human civilization. House-building on earth is in imitation of Enki's act as "he drew the line, arranged the foundations, he built the house beside the council and arranged the rites of purification, the great ruler laid the foundation walls (and) set the bricks on them. The one whose foundation walls set in the earth will never shift, whose well-built house will never totter, whose well-established roof reaches to heaven. . . ."[3]

The contrast between the two fundamental human activities, the former one demanding intelligence rather than will, and the latter will rather than intelligence, found a dramatic and profound illustration in early history. In the background is a matriarchal type of society that may have preceded patriarchy. Indeed, the earliest evidence of human religious activity points to the generalized worship of the goddess. In the Upper Paleolithic levels (25,000 to 8000 B.C.E.) archaeology has discovered numerous female statuettes that leave no doubt about the wide extent of the cult of the Mother Goddess, patron of fertility and fecundity. That state of things became ever clearer with the Mesolithic age (8000 to 4000 B.C.E.) and the Neolithic (4000 to 2500 B.C.E.). But, during the second and third millennia, far-reaching historical commotions occurred that made the pendulum swing dramatically to the other extreme. I am referring to waves of Indo-European peoples that flooded the countries between the Two Rivers. Those Indo-Europeans probably worshiped volcanoes (because of the impressive association of mountain and fire). At any rate, their divinities were male gods, and their unstoppable conquest of other nations was not surprisingly interpreted as signifying the superiority of gods over goddesses, hence of maleness over femaleness. This explains why, at the dawn of the historical era and for millennia since, women in the ancient Near East were relegated to minor religious roles. The exceptions to this rule only emphasize the gravity of the general phenomenon.

---

3. See *Near Eastern Religious Texts Relating to the Old Testament,* ed. Walter Beyerlin, 80.

There were, for instance, females among the scribes of Babylonia. Very impressive is the case at the end of the third millennium of the Akkadian princess Enheduanna; she is the first known author in world literature. At Mari on the Euphrates, some women were prominent as prophets. In general, however, it was considered a privilege for women to belong to the lower clergy as singers, dancers, musicians, or sacred prostitutes.

THE WOMAN IN ISRAEL

Yahwism in Israel describes a socioreligious situation similar to that in the ancient Near East. For centuries Yahwism struggled to suppress goddess worship altogether, be it Asherah, Anath, or Ishtar-Astarte. Israel no less than the other nations in the region was a patriarchal society. It is against that background, common to the whole of the ancient Middle East, that we must examine any possible distinctiveness of Israel. A hint to such a possibility is provided by the very fact that "Israel" is the name given to an egalitarian social body in contrast with the feudal societies of the region. Norman Gottwald, in his celebrated book *The Tribes of Yahweh* (Maryknoll: Orbis Books, 1979), coins the term "Mono-Yahwism" to describe the fact that YHWH is equally the god of all members of the federation united by covenant. One could, therefore, expect that the ideal of equality would be extended to the relationships between sexes. In fact, however, many external phenomena belie that expectation. Besides, modern sociologists of the Bible insist upon a greater closeness with the Canaanite formal structure than was generally admitted.

In Israel as well, for example, the extended family is called *beith-ab* (literally, "the father's home"), and the federation as a whole is organized around the (male) heads of families. Thus, the nation delegates its collective power to the elders (Deut. 21:1-9; 25:7-10; Ruth 4:2). During the postexilic era, the texts speak of male assemblies making decisions that involve the whole of the community and, sometimes directly or even cruelly, the female element in its midst (see Ezra 10).

The status of the woman is fundamentally tied with property ownership (see Exod. 20:17; Deut. 5:21). A *beith-ab* exchanges women with another *beith-ab*. Such transactions presuppose a minimum of peaceful relations, for negotiations before marriage are often complicated. The group that receives a woman from another is considered to be indebted to the providing group until the former can reciprocate. Marriage, at any rate, is a covenant, not just between two persons, but between two groups. Because marriage is not privatized, it provides social security for women, with provisions for widows and orphans, neither of whose care is a private matter (cf. Ruth). By the same token, marriage is a way to regulate sexual behavior and to channel it toward procreation and legitimation of children.

Sex is here ambivalent. In reaction against Canaanite license paradoxically based on the sacralization of sex, there was in Israel a "demythization" of sexuality, now understood as participation in divine creation, communication and communion between the two genders, and the means of perpetuating life (see Gen. 1:26-31). But sex is highly vulnerable and susceptible of being perverted. It serves its purpose only when kept in check (like the tongue of which James speaks in the New Testament). Hence, a hedge is built around sexual behavior; the laws are detailed and specific about that aspect of human life (see, for example, Deut. 22:13-21; Lev. 15:19-30; 18:6-18,22; 20:10; Exod. 22:19). Marriage, therefore, is also a discipline to which all should submit. The absence of romanticism in the Israelite conception of that institution is particularly clear in a custom like the levirate marriage, with which the book of Ruth will give us ample opportunity to deal.

Before we turn to highly interesting reactions in specific milieus of Israel against the prevailing situation, a few correctives belonging to the general picture must be cited. First, there is a wholehearted acknowledgement of *love* and of its determinant nature, especially for the woman in marriage (see Gen. 24:67; 29:20; 34:3ff.; 1 Sam. 1:8). The mother is deeply respected (see Deut. 27:16; Lev. 20:9). Sages delight in describing "women of valor" and how great a blessing it is to deal with such exceptional persons (the word *exceptional* is here to be taken in its dual meaning as far as wisdom literature is concerned). In the book of Proverbs the importance of the enthusiastic praise of the "strong woman" in 31:10ff. is underscored by its placement as the conclusion of the entire book. In the Apocrypha, there are numerous echoes of that sentiment, two of which are books that we shall examine here, Susanna and Judith (see also Sir. 26:13-18; 2 Macc. 7:20ff.).

Under the influence of the prophets, the great compositions of traditions in the Tetrateuch have granted to sexuality a choice place in their conceptions of human existence under God. J, in Gen. 2:23, shows sexuality as created simultaneously for male and female. The rule of man over woman is a sign of the perversion of creation by the human couple (see Gen. 3:16). E, in Gen. 15:4, has the daring image of a parturient Abraham (see Vg.: *"qui egredietur de utero tuo"!* [the one who comes out of your own womb]). Similarly, P brings his story of creation before the Sabbath day to a climax with these powerful words: "And God created the human in his own image, in the image of God created he him, male and female created he them" (Gen. 1:27).

In the prophetic books themselves are found striking metaphors that say a great deal about the broad-mindedness of the prophets on that score. Their use of feminine imagery to describe God's feelings for his people, for example, reveals their amazing freedom of thought, especially when it is realized how vehement they are in their denunciations of their people's idolatry, particularly that which involves feminine deities. Texts like Isa. 42:13f.; 49:14f.; and 66:12f., among others, are to be cited (see also Deut. 32:18). Hosea 2:16-18 announces the coming harmony between the divine husband and the human partner, who is here feminine. In chapter 11, the prophet describes the loving care, indeed the motherly care, with which God has treated his people.

The amazing text of Jer. 31:22 reads, "For the Lord creates a new thing on the earth [or: in the land], the woman encompasses the man." William L. Holladay has written a convincing study of this mysterious text.[4] He first calls attention to the assonance between the verb *tesobeb* (encompasses) and *hashobebah* (backsliding [daughter]) in the same verse. "To encompass" is again

---

4. William L. Holladay, "Jeremiah XXXI 22b reconsidered: 'The Woman encompasses the man.'"

found in Deut. 32:10 *(yesobebenhu)* with the idea that YHWH encompasses or embraces Israel; that is, grants Israel his protective dominance. In order fully to savor the Jeremian text, one must remember that the word *neqebah* (woman, female) has the etymological meaning "concave" (we shall return to this below), and is here in close proximity to the verb *bara'* (create), thus forming a striking parallel to Gen. 1:27, quoted above. The meaning of the prophetic sentence is, therefore, the following: God is going to redo his creation, and now the female/concave will protect the warrior (literal sense of *geber,* which here replaces *zakhar* of Genesis 1). The background of the statement is the taunt so often used to offend the enemy before battle: they are but women! (see Jer. 49:22; 50:37; 51:30; Nah. 3:13). Israel has been humiliated by the Babylonians, but now YHWH withdraws the curse. He makes a new creation, reversing the sex roles. If the warriors became women in the eyes of Babylon, women will now dominate over warriors. One cannot but think of Mother Arnauld of Port-Royal des Champs when she replied to threats on the part of ecclesiastical authorities, *"Si les évêques ont des courages de femmes, les femmes auront des courages d'évêques"* (If bishops are only as tough as women, women will be as tough as bishops).

In what follows, we shall encounter at least a couple of those "women who encompass warriors." Esther puts her life on the line and confronts her redoubtable husband to save her people. Judith goes alone to the heart of the enemy camp, where no Israelite hero dared go. She fulfills her mission by beheading Holofernes, thus symbolically castrating the "macho."

Along the same line, but in a much more subtle way, the story of Ruth is a pamphlet of feminist theology. The author has unevenly distributed the roles of the characters. All of the males but one are hostile to Naomi and Ruth. None of them but Boaz is named in the story, at least if one excludes the patrilinear genealogy at the end (4:18-22), which is perhaps inauthentic and in any case is clearly outside the story proper. Strikingly, the Matthean genealogy of Jesus, based in part upon the genealogy in Ruth, restores the names of several women in the list (see chapter 6 below).

In summary, Israel had dissonant voices. They stress all the more the discrepancy between the revolutionary program of the nation of Israel liberating itself from the dictatorship of feudal city-states in Canaan, and, on the other hand, the status of women, which, according to law and custom, remained, as it were, unliberated in a patriarchal society. Here again, socioeconomic studies shed light on this paradoxical situation. Particularly helpful is Carol L. Meyers.[5] Meyers reminds the reader of the frequent outbreaks of violence during the Late Bronze Age, which also contributed to natural insecurity caused in large part by frightening eruptions of epidemics. In this context, the prophetic threats of "famine, pestilence, and sword" all take their relevance. It seems that the death rate required that a couple produce twice as many children as would survive infancy. One-third of the individuals died before the age of five; one-half did not survive beyond eighteen. A much greater number of women died than men. Meyers writes, "Women in antiquity were a class of humanity in short supply."[6] This acute situation persisted until the central Middle Ages, when there was a reversal in the proportion of female and male deaths.

With the Israelite conquest/liberation in the thirteenth century B.C.E., the future of Israel depended in large part upon populating the land (see Exod. 23:23-30). Significant is the fact that originally they settled in uninhabited hilly territories (demanding new devices such as terracing and new tools of iron).[7] On the enemy side, the situation was no less somber. Archaeology shows that one after the other of the city-states suffered violent destruction (not necessarily by the hand of the Israelites). Meyers advances the idea that the explanation may be a kind of "desperate public health measure" in parallel with the later medieval quarantines that at times involved entire cities.

In other words, survival demanded reproduction; and, since females were in short supply, they had to be protected from the dangers of hunt and war. The family was the vital nucleus tightly

---

5. Carol L. Meyers, "The Roots of Restriction: Women in Early Israel," 289–306; see also id., *Discovering Eve.*
6. Meyers, "The Roots of Restriction," 295.
7. See Meyers, *Discovering Eve,* chapter 3.

gathered around females, who, in addition to their invaluable biological functions, would also participate in the chores of a land-based economy. From such a perspective, Exod. 20:12 ("Honor your father and your mother, that your days may be long . . .") gains a more practical tone! Similarly, Num. 31:18 illustrates the severity of the situation. The virgins are first kept in quarantine while they purify their bodies, clothes, and belongings. Religious motives here go hand in hand with health requirements. The same book indicates that 14,700 died at the start of a plague that erupted in the Israelite camp (16:49).

Against that background, one can understand why Meyers calls it "an irony of history" that the "tight channeling of female (and male) energies into domestic affairs, which was a liberating event in its own time," became institutionalized as a pattern of female behavior "in ways that became limiting and oppressive to women."[8] Some, however, felt the necessity to react against an evolving degradation, and to retrieve the time of Israel's childhood, the time of the desert wandering, when God "led them with humane cords and with bands of love" (Hos. 11:4). It is of utmost importance to realize that a return to the pristine premonarchic ideal is advocated during the Second Temple period by texts that must be dubbed a literature of protest. The books with which this essay deals, Susanna, Esther, Ruth, and Judith, all date from that period and belong to that category. We could also add to these documents the Song of Songs, which "depict[s] a kind of harmonious ideal or balance between the sexes."[9] Suffice it here to refer to Song 2:16; 6:3; 7:10[11]. Characteristically, at the end of the book of Job—another "antiestablishment" pamphlet—the seven sons of Job remain anonymous, but his daughters are named, and they inherit from their father like the sons!

Over and beyond the institutionalized barriers set up by law and custom—originally with the best of intentions, in particular for the protection of the female reproductive capacities vital for society's survival—women in Israel such as the matriarchs, the Miriams and Ruths, Deborahs and Jaels, Esthers and Judiths,

8. Meyers, "The Roots of Restriction," 295.
9. Ibid., 303.

and many others with them, were living reminders that the equality of women was not only a possibility contemplated by dreamers and by isolated texts in the Bible, but an integral part of the religious, social, economical, and political movement of liberation called *Israel.*

MALENESS AND FEMALENESS IN THE NARRATIVES ON CREATION IN GENESIS

In the book of Zohar (2.3a) one can read this amazing statement:

> This king [the third Sefirah, i.e., Binah, intelligence], although he is a supreme king, is female in relation to the supreme point [the second Sefirah, i.e., Hokhmah, wisdom] which is completely hidden. But though female, he is male in relation to the lower king [the sixth Sefirah, Tiph'eret, beauty (or) compassion].

This text is important for the topic of this chapter, because it clearly interprets the genders as contingent instead of absolute, as relational instead of self-contained. The same being can be male *in relation to* someone or something, and female *in relation to* another. I shall try to show in this section that the interpretation of reality by the text of the Zohar above is correct with regard to the Genesis narratives on "the beginning."

We already noted that in Jeremiah 31 the basic meaning of *neqebah,* female, is "concave." The term is used in Genesis 1 for designating "Eve," while "Adam" is *zakhar,* male; that is, "convex." Thus P makes it crystal-clear that a complete human being is both male and female, as the same geometrical figure is both convex and concave according to the perspective of the onlooker. The complementarity of both aspects of the same complex allows P to stress their contrasting sameness and dissimilarity, a true condition for a living relationship between the two (Gen. 1:27a; cf. 2:23; 1:27b; 2:20,23). The one is what the other is not, but the one is what he is *in relation to,* thanks to, and for the sake of the other, and vice versa. Maleness exists only when facing femaleness, and femaleness when facing maleness. The genders are less biological data than historical, dynamic means of communication.

With *zakhar,* the accent is on productive creativity of Adam in the image of God's creative activity. With *neqebah,* the accent is on creative receptivity in the image of God's creative "reflection." "God saw that it was good . . ." (this we could also understand as meaning that he saw to it that it be good, i.e., capable of fulfilling its vocation).

Remarkably enough, modern theories of communication insist on basic conditions that recall very closely what the creation narratives in Genesis understand as the relation between the sexes. It is stressed today that for communication to happen, there must be at least two communicators. The message is sent and received, hence there are a sender and a receiver, but the roles are not that clear-cut; *the sender is also the receiver, and the receiver is also the sender.* The sender sends the message always in response to what he has received. That is why the Creator God transcends maleness and femaleness: if the sender is called convex and the receiver concave, then God is neither and both, for he sends messages that he did not receive in the first place but rather created, and nonetheless remains open to receive response to his message.

Richard Crable sums up the process of communication in the following way: "These phases of the process are important for both or all of the participants involved in the communication."[10] The message that finally results from the sender's reception, interpretation, choice, symbolization, and transmission becomes something the receiver receives as a stimulus. The receiver receives the verbal or nonverbal stimulus, and then must interpret the message. A choice is made, and the chosen response is symbolized and transmitted to the person who first sent the message. The result is feedback, and the original sender now acts as a receiver. These activities can be "viewed as a process since they can go indefinitely and simultaneously; they can be viewed as a transaction because both or all the participants are affected and changed by the process that occurs."

One could also think of the relationship between convex and concave in terms of outwardness (convexity, outreach) and in-

10. Richard Crable, *Using Communication,* 19.

wardness (concavity, receptivity). In literature, for example, the inwardness of *neqebah* is expressed by a characterization through interior monologue. Women are depicted as being in love, in crisis, torn between loyalty and passion, not able to confide in anyone, contemplating suicide. R. Scholes and R. Kellogg cite as examples Medea, Dido, Anna Karenina, Molly Bloom. . . .[11] For Claude Lévi-Strauss the only difference irreducible to structuration is the one between man and woman, source of all disorder. According to the myths, culture belongs to man and nature to woman, but "what man taught to woman as a lesson, woman will live it in the blooming of her physiological functions. Man culturalizes, so to speak, what used to be nature; woman naturalizes what used to be culture. In passing from man to woman, the verb became flesh."[12]

Be that as it may, in the creation narratives of Genesis the woman, called *neqebah* by P, is named *hawwah* (Eve) by J, for, says 3:20, "she is the mother of all living." The verb indeed means "alive," and the *neqebah* is thus described as being life and bringing forth life. She is creator with the whole of her being. Wherever she goes, she is nest for life. Her very name spells life. Hence the strange statement by J that "a man shall leave his father and his mother, and he shall cleave unto his wife, and they shall be one flesh" (again, we could say).

J also has a name for the *zakhar:* Adam (which thus passes from the status of a noun to that of a name). Adam is in charge of gardening; his function is husbandry. He becomes creative to the very extent that he performs according to his vocation. He is *homo faber* in compensation for his lack on the level of being. While Eve is what she *is,* Adam is what he *does.* Adam, by necessity, must become *homo economicus.* His raison d'être is to organize and reorganize goods and tasks. It is a truism that for a merchant everything has a commercial value. Trade means the transmission of the ownership of goods. It is based on the moving of riches, of values. It is not surprising, therefore, that for *homo economicus* woman becomes the bartering good par excellence.

11. R. Scholes and R. Kellogg, *The Nature of Narrative,* 182–83.
12. Claude Lévi-Strauss, *L'origine des manières de table,* 249, au. trans.

Moreover, one must keep in mind that in a premonetary system of economy the objects for bartering are not appraised according to their real commercial value but according to their virtues, especially the supernatural ones, granted to them by both partners of the transaction. One should keep this important point in mind and not jump to overstated conclusions when reading texts such as Gen. 31:15; 34:12 (cf. Exod. 22:16; 1 Sam. 18:25); Deut. 22:29. . . . It remains true that in a bartering economy women figure high on the list of the most desirable "possessions."

That Israel was able—even though at times only and in a certain spiritual elite only—to transcend the economic dimension so deeply anchored in the patriarchal type of society is nothing short of miraculous. In the narratives that we shall study here, women are much more than economic objects: they become the central characters, the heroines, of decisive events in the history of their people. They are, as we shall see, put on a par with the greatest patriarchs of the past (see Ruth). Their virtues surpass by far those of their male contemporaries, who sometimes are described as sheer scoundrels (see Susanna). They muster the courage of generals, while the generals recoil in their burrows (see Judith). They show such a contempt for riches and honors, so dearly treasured by their male fellows, as to consider them as nothing for the sake of the survival of their people (see Esther). The process of liberation of a people is complete only when women and men reach equality. This lesson was taught in Israel, either by good men who created literary heroines as mouthpieces for the message or by female authors whose plea was so earnestly heeded that their poems were deemed worthy of being canonized.

CHAPTER 3

Susanna

For practical reasons we turn first to the story of Susanna. It is the shortest and also the simplest of the four documents. In the Greek versions of the Old Testament it precedes the first chapter of Daniel and introduces Daniel as a "child." In Syriac tradition the story is sometimes called "The Book of Little Daniel." It is not without importance to note the many Semitisms in the Greek. This very fact renders untenable the opinion[1] that a Hebrew *Vorlage* is unlikely because of the wordplay in the Greek of vv. 54f. and 58f. Modern translators have shown repeatedly that in those passages, an original wordplay is readily rendered by a wordplay in the reception language.

The story is about a virtuous Jewess in exile in Babylon. Two Jewish elders attempt to force her to commit adultery. Unsuccessful, they accuse her of their own crime. She is being led to death, on the ground of the elders' accusation and without further inquiry, but she is rescued by the child Daniel, who demonstrates the elders' perjury and calumny. They are put to death.

Susanna has been variously judged by critics. Cappelus in the seventeenth century called it *"fabula ineptissima"* (a very silly fable), but modern scholars are a great deal more positive. Bruce Metzger calls it one of "the best stories in the world's literature."[2] Carey Moore stresses the success of the story, describing it as "a

---

1. Repeated by E. Kamlah in *Biblisch-Historisches Handwörterbuch* III (1896).
2. Bruce Metzger, *An Introduction to the Apocrypha,* 107. J. de Menasce concurs, Introduction to Daniel, *Bible de Jérusalem,* 19.

skillful admixture of three of the most basic and universal fascinations of man: God, sex, and death."[3]

This takes us to the question of literary genre. We are dealing with a folktale whose obvious biblical parallel is afforded by the judgment of Solomon. (In both cases, note that the whole point is made at the end of the story.) Origen already compares the child Daniel's capacity to Solomon's in 1 Kings 3:16ff. This Elias Bickerman contrasts with Julius Africanus' judgment (ca. 230 C.E.) seeing in Susanna a "romance" comparable to Greek comedies. Africanus' opinion is supported, continues Bickerman, by the fact that indeed the scene of Susanna's bath in the garden exists only in the later version of Theodotion but is absent in the Septuagint (vv. 7-8: ". . . Susanna went into her husband's garden to walk. And the two elders saw her going in every day and walking.")[4]

There are also nonbiblical parallels.[5] There is even a marginal story in "The Thousand and One Nights" that is analogous to our tale. In every such narrative, there is a last-minute intervention by a young child who displays great wisdom and restores justice. The kinship between these folktales matches especially the third scene of Susanna, where the accent is on the wonder of a very young boy wiser than the sages.

But those Oriental stories are generally not about unjustly accused women as here in the first two scenes of Susanna. These belong to the so-called Genoveva type, examples of which are found in the stories of Joseph accused by the wife of Potiphar and of Hippolytus accused by Phaedra, among others. "Genoveva" is the chaste wife falsely accused, usually by an unsuccessful suitor.[6] The woman slandered as adulteress may be thrown into a den of lions, who do not harm her. The story of Susanna, however, contains several variations of that type. While there is generally one rejected suitor, here there are two. The reason is that accord-

---

3. C. A. Moore, *Daniel, Esther, and Jeremiah: The Additions,* 78.
4. E. Bickerman, *The Jews in the Greek Age,* 95.
5. G. Huet has gathered several of them in "Daniel et Susanne: Note de littérature comparée."
6. Cf. Stith Thompson, *The Motif-Index of Folk-Literature,* 4:474, ad K:2, 112, "woman slandered as adulteress [prostitute]"; Crescentia, Genoveva, Susanna . . . ad B:522.3.

ing to Jewish law, two witnesses are a minimum to instruct a judgment leading to capital punishment (Deut. 17:6).

Second, Genesis 39 (Joseph and Potiphar's wife) most certainly served as the model for our tale. But the male and female roles are reversed. Thus we learn from v. 12 that the elders "day by day" watched Susanna; in Gen. 39:10, Joseph is spoken to by his master's wife, "day by day." In v. 23a, Susanna refuses "to sin against the Lord"; in Gen. 39:9, similarly, Joseph refuses to "sin against God." In v. 26, the household rushes in to see what happened to Susanna; in Gen. 39:14ff., Potiphar's wife summons the people of the household to denounce Joseph's attempt to rape her. In v. 39, Susanna's alleged paramour escaped the elders who could not hold him; in Gen. 39:18, Joseph allegedly dodged his victim's attempt to detain him. In Joseph's story, the evidence is Joseph's robe; in Susanna's, it is the woman herself (Gen. 39:12, 18, and Susanna, v. 40). This inspired John Chrysostom to the following reflection: "Susanna endured a severe fight, more severe than that of Joseph. He, a man, contended with one woman, but Susanna, a woman, had to contend with two men, and was a spectacle to men and to angels."[7] The contrast is further strengthened by the fact that Susanna has no title of nobility but her personal virtue. In the words of George Nickelsburg, "The old court tale has been democratized. The heroine is not a sage but an ordinary, God-fearing person. Her enemies are not a king or his courtiers but Jewish compatriots."[8]

When such reversals of pattern occur, the conclusion is almost certain that a traditional scene has been borrowed by a polemicist to make a point. The method used is very close to the hermeneutical Rabbinic rule called *ribbuy u-miyut* (from extension to reduction), or to the one called *qelal u-perat* (from general to particular). In other words, the author uses an a fortiori argument: If the traditional scene is convincing as is, it is even more so when the characters are poetically changed "downward," from a sage to an ordinary person, from an Israelite to a Moabite, or in

---

7. Sermon on Susanna, quoted by Metzger, *Introduction to the Apocrypha*, 112.
8. G. W. E. Nickelsburg, *Jewish Literature between the Bible and the Mishnah*, 26. He adds, "Thus the confrontation between Jew and foreigner, essential to Daniel 1–6, is lacking here."

a patriarchal society, from a hero to a heroine. The same result obtains when the foe is changed "upward," from a heathen to a Jew. Similarly, place settings can change without damage to the story's lesson—for example, from Egypt to Babylon. In addition, the process of democratization takes the reader not only from royal court to marketplace, from kings to commoners, and, in terms of plot, from the epic to the novelistic, but also from the men's world to the women's world. This latter phenomenon is so striking that in the Jacobite Syriac version, the four books "of the women" are usually grouped together, thus Susanna is joined with Ruth, Esther, and Judith. Furthermore, it is noteworthy that "Shoshanah" (Susanna) does not appear elsewhere in the Old Testament as a name; it occurs frequently, however, as a noun in Song of Songs. "We may conclude," says Louis Hartman, "that the heroine of the story is given the name 'Lily' to evoke the delightful freshness and surpassing beauty of the beloved woman in the Song of Songs."[9] Thus is completed a "pentateuchal" series of books "of the women." All these books, with the possible exception of the Song of Songs, belong to the underground Jewish literature of the Second Temple period.

This brings us to the problem of the story's objective. In 1877, N. Brüll suggested that Susanna was a Pharisaic pamphlet of the first century B.C.E. attacking the court procedures of the Sadducees. Such a clash between the two sects on the subject of court judgments is documented by *Pirke Aboth* 1:10 (1:9). There, the Pharisee Simeon ben Shetah argues for the cross-examination of witnesses.[10] Perjury by witnesses must be fought by inflicting on the perjurer the penalty he sought to inflict on the accused, and by leaving alone the innocent (cf. Deut. 19:19). It is told that R. Simeon's son, although innocent in a judgment, chose death so that his father might inflict the capital penalty on the Sadducees,

9. L. F. Hartman and A. A. DiLella, *The Book of Daniel*, 20.

10. The setting is the rulership of Alexander Janneus (102–75 B.C.E.). See also *m. Sanh.* 5:2; *Sanh.* 41a. For N. Brüll, the background of Susanna is a legend built on Jer. 29:21-23. The false prophets Ahab and Zedekiah there were later identified by Jewish tradition as Susanna's elders (especially in *Midrash Tanhuma,* where both are thrown into fire by Nebuchadnezzar [cf. Jer. 29:22] along with the high priest Joshua ben Yotsadak). This tradition was known by Origen and Jerome. See N. Brüll, "Das apokryphische Susanna Buch."

his false accusers. In Susanna, the death penalty is ultimately meted out on the wicked elders.

But the counter-arguments to Brüll's theory are all but irresistible. There is here no "Sadducee" judge. The atmosphere is too tumultuous and improper to make a juridical point. Daniel is not the adept judge but the inspired sage. The elders are condemned *before* their hearing; certainly a questionable juridical procedure! Furthermore, as S. B. Hoenig points out,[11] had the book been anti-Sadducee, it would have been included in the (Pharisaic) canon. But in fact, the Pharisaic law on the death penalty for false witness is based on a "matter of time" (alibi), and not, as in Susanna, on the contradiction of "witnesses in fact." Not only was the story not canonized by the Pharisees, but traces of it in Jewish literature are, at best, discreet. *Leviticus Rabba* 19 reports a story that may constitute a parallel: Nebuchadnezzar's wife—it is said—interceded for Jehoiachin's wife that she be permitted to visit her husband in prison and have intercourse with him (to prevent the extinction of the house of David). When she came into the prison, she said, "I've seen as it were a red lily *(shushanah),"* meaning, "I have my menses." In keeping with the Torah, the king did not approach her (cf. Lev. 15:19-30; 18:19; 20:18). Now if, in accord with that Haggadah, "shushanah" is to be taken in Susanna symbolically or etiologically, it is interesting that Susanna's husband is called Joakim, a name similar to that of King Jehoiachin (see 2 Kings 24:8,12; 1 Esdras 1:43), also called Jechonias in Greek (Baruch 1:3; Jer. 22:24 var.; 2 Chron. 36:8f.), that is, the king in exile in Babylon. Strikingly, in *The Book of Jerahmeel* (eleventh century)—of which more will be said later—Susanna is both the granddaughter and the wife of King Jehoiachin (a union forbidden by Lev. 18:10!). Similarly, in the Ethiopian Falashic version (see below), Susanna is the daughter of a king and the widow of a king. The tradition was known by Origen, Jerome, Hippolytus, and Georgius Syncellus.[12]

That Susanna is not just a commoner is clear from the story's setting, which suggests she belongs to a well-to-do family. The

11. S. B. Hoenig, "Susanna," 467f.
12. *Chronographia,* pp. 218f., in *Corpus Scriptorum Historiae Byzantinae* VI, 1, 413.

nobility of her behavior points in the same direction. The child Daniel emphasizes that she is "a woman of Israel" (v. 48), even "a woman of Judah," a category that he places on a higher echelon than the "women of Israel" (v. 57). The motif is somewhat surprising. It echoes, of course, the deep divisions that plagued the Second Temple commonwealth. The name "Israel" had become in Jerusalem a dubious title. The northern ten tribes, it was thought, had not been found worthy of restoration; and neighboring "Samaria" was now considered a nest of syncretism. But such a characterization smacks of the ideology of the conservative party. Here, in the mouth of Daniel, it is unexpected. One possible solution is that Daniel's objectivity is stressed. He does not come to the rescue of the woman, but of the righteous (here identified with "Judah"). If such be the case, it would definitely distance Susanna from being understood as a feminist pamphlet. On the other hand, Daniel's remark may be ironic. He may be using categories favored by the bourgeois, but those complacent classifications backfire, for the elders then happen to be guilty of the character assassination of people they consider to be saintly!

Very little can be drawn from the Samaritan version, the Falashic version, and *The Book of Jerahmeel*. The Samaritan version of Susanna was influenced by Christianity.[13] The action occurred, it says, "in the days of the sixth high priest after the appearance of Joshua son of Miriam, the carpenter's wife." It is the story of the daughter of Amram, the Samaritan high priest. She lived as a *nazir* (Nazirite) and was accused by frustrated men of fornication. But the high priest proved that they were false witnesses. As such, they were executed by fire. (According to Lev. 21:9, the penalty for fornication on the part of a priest's daughter is death by fire, not by stoning. Here, therefore, the false witnesses die by fire, according to the rule spelled out in Deut. 19:19, "Then shall you do to [the false witness] as he had meant to do to his brother.")

Max Wurmbrand has translated and commented on the Ethiopic text, "A Falasha Variant of Susanna."[14] As in the other tex-

---

13. It was presented by R. Adler and M. Seligson in 1903, *Une nouvelle chronique samaritaine*, 42–44.
14. M. Wurmbrand, "A Falasha Variant of Susanna." It is Ms. 8 of the Faitlovitch Library of Tel Aviv, titled "The Acts of Susanna."

tual traditions, the heroine's kin here are all royal. Widowed, she would not remarry, she said: "I have devoted myself to the Lord, my creator." When we turn to the story of Judith, we shall see that she too was widowed and kept mourning and fasting instead of remarrying (8:5ff.). Three elders tried to lie with Susanna, "but she signed her face three times with the sign of the Lord." Then the elders slandered her to her father, saying that she fornicated "with everybody." Her father threw her in a pit but the archangel Michael came down to her "in the semblance of a man." Then Michael went to the king, who had the elders questioned to find out under what tree the crime was committed and at what time in the day. Susanna was vindicated and made queen. Or, as the text says, she was rewarded with "queenship on earth and bliss in heaven."

The Book of Jerahmeel (eleventh century C.E.) was translated into English by Moses Gaster in 1899.[15] *Jerahmeel* was considered by Gaster as the Semitic *Vorlage* of Susanna. In fact, the work is a Hebrew translation of the text of the Vulgate, itself based on the Greek version of Theodotion.

All those variants of our story show how popular the tale of Susanna has been, first among Christians and later among Jews (who were influenced by the former, as is clear from the Samaritan and the Falashic versions).[16] The parallel stories shed light on the objective of the "original" tale. Wurmbrand, for instance, suggested an interesting *Sitz im Leben.* "This," he wrote, "was possibly a story told by the Palestinian Am Ha-aretz who through Susanna's mouth expressed their rancour against the intellectual aristocracy of the Rabbis."[17] This statement puts us on the right track, I believe. Already Julius Africanus, more than two centuries after the time of Jesus, compared the story with the mimographer Philiston, who used to expose his contemporaries' hidden sins ruthlessly. A subversive piece of literature, Susanna satirizes the Jewish "establishment." It contrasts the virtuous

15. *Chronicles of Jerahmeel,* ed. M. Gaster.
16. Let us here mention a late Jewish parallel to our story. When Joseph was flogged for allegedly attempting to rape "Zuleika," her babe of but eleven months had his mouth opened by God and said, "what is your quarrel with this man?" and the infant denounced the lies of his mother (*Yashar Wayesheb* 88a–89a [seventeenth century]).
17. Wurmbrand, "Falasha Variant," 30.

Jewess Susanna with lecherous elders, and wise children with aged scoundrels. To the extent that the book of Daniel is itself the fruit of the party of opposition in Jerusalem, the story of Susanna, from a sociological perspective, has its place with that book.[18]

From a literary point of view, however, C. A. Moore considers Susanna ill fitted for the book of Daniel. This would be one reason why the story was not received into the Rabbinic canon. Another ground, as seen earlier, would be that the story allegedly contradicts a rule of the Mishnah on witnesses.[19] For Origen, its exclusion was due to details discreditable to the Jewish nation. He was followed by Hippolytus (third century). The fact is that there is no attestation of Susanna in Qumran or in the writings of Josephus, and very little in Rabbinic literature before the eleventh century. On the other hand, as says D. M. Kay,

> had there been no Hebrew original, it is difficult to see why Symmachus and Theodotion should have taken the trouble to revise a casual tract. . . . The second century A. D. produced versions enough to secure a place for Susanna in the Tetrapla of Origen ca. A. D. 240 . . . [but] the story would not be popular with elders, and it was elders who fixed the Canon.[20]

We come full circle to the critique of elders in the story. True, there are in the Rabbinic canon texts with similar criticism (cf. 1 Kings 21; Jer. 23:15 [LXX 29:21-23].) But the denunciation of the "establishment" is much more pointed in our story than in Ruth or Jonah, for instance, and this, I believe, is the true reason why Susanna was left out. As writes J. de Menasce, the polemics "could possibly be against the Second Temple era priests, to whom would be opposed the clear-sighted candor of the inspired child, of the prophet of old."[21]

Generally that type of literature describes how God himself comes to the defense of the righteous.[22] In this particular case,

18. See my *Daniel in His Time.*
19. *m. Sanh.* 5:1, "matter of time," alibi.
20. D. M. Kay, in *APOT,* 1:642.
21. J. de Menasce, "Daniel," 19 (my translation).
22. So the story of Ahikar, Wisdom of Solomon 2-5, Tobit, Judith, the Additions to Esther, and Daniel 1-6.

the exclusive redeeming role of YHWH is stressed by the unworthiness and improbability of the human agent. Daniel seems but a child, but to God he is a prophet and a sage.

This point is important, for with the pairing of Susanna and Daniel, the story emphasizes the conjunction of righteousness and wisdom. The righteous is accompanied by a sage that "makes wise," by a wise one that "justifies many" (Dan. 12:3). Our sense of wonder increases when the sage is a child, for thus it is stressed that the source of his wisdom is a gift of the Spirit. Because of this, Daniel can mete out a judgment against the elders before any proof of guilt is produced, moved as he is by his prophetic inspiration.

On this score alone the story was bound to displease scribal Judaism, for which prophecy had ceased with Haggai, Zechariah, and Malachi. No prophetic source of authority could any longer be claimed, for the exegetes or "doctors of the Law" were now "sitting on Moses' seat" succeeding and replacing him. "Free" inspiration had increasingly been considered with suspicion (cf. Zech. 13:2-6), until it was all but suppressed as spurious. Judaism is a postprophetic phenomenon. Its inspiration is less charismatic than it is *halakic* (legalistic). What is inspired is the tradition (written and oral). The scribe is its interpreter. As is typical in the history of thought, later developments are retrojected onto the past. Early Judaism came to see history as a succession of generations led by their contemporary interpreters: *"dor, dor, wedoreshayw"* (all generations with their interpreters), as the Rabbis say.

In consequence, a story of the second or first century B.C.E. that told of an inspired child teaching the guardians of tradition[23] would have to have had a polemical aim and a subversive message. Not only does Susanna's story not deal with court procedures on which Pharisees and Sadducees diverged (see above), but it questions the legalistic bent of the one and the other. Religious authority does not lie in skillful exegesis, the appanage of the scribes, but in the Spirit that blows where it pleases.[24] To

---

23. A motif discretely picked up by the Gospel; see Luke 2:46ff.
24. Cf. Matt. 7:29; Mark 1:22; John 3:8; Matt. 13:54; Luke 4:14ff.; Mark 12:35.

the ideology of the institution, Susanna opposes the utopia of the event. The Law is not averse to this. That is why Torah occupies a central position here. Death is preferable to transgressing it (vv. 3, 23). It is the great authority (v. 62), taught by parents to children (v. 3). Who does not live according to the prescriptions of the Torah is unworthy to have a part in the community; he or she is unworthy of life. So far, the Rabbis were in full agreement. But there is a twist. The bête noire in Susanna is not a minor member of society like a woman, but a pair of elders or scribes on whose authority the community relies. They covet and are adulterous (v. 41), they bring a false accusation (v. 62), they put upon themselves bloodguilt (vv. 48, 50), they disregard the innocent (v. 60). They are the wicked (v. 62).

There can be little doubt that the boomeranging accusation in the tale of Susanna provided a spiritual and possibly a literary model for certain denunciations of the "establishment" by Jesus. Using parallel categories, he stressed the hypocrisy of religious leaders who beheld the straw in others' eyes but not the beam in their own, and who in general put upon others' shoulders heavy burdens that they would not even touch with a finger (Matt. 7:3; Luke 11:46).

Or, if one prefers an example from secular literature, a quote from Lucian in the second century c.e. will do. In a parody of the philosophers' discourse, Lucian says, "If a rich man keeps a costly table or a mistress, I make it my business to be properly horrified; but if my familiar friend is lying sick, in need of help and care, I am not aware of it."[25]

---

25. Lucian, *Icaromenippus,* trans. H. W. Fowler (Oxford: Clarendon, 1905), para. 31.

CHAPTER 4

Judith

Nebuchadnezzar (LXX: Nabuchodonodor) is one of the most infamous characters of the Bible. He is that Babylonian king who in the sixth century B.C.E. captured Jerusalem, pillaged it, burned the Temple, and exiled much of the Judaean population to Mesopotamia. He is introduced in Judith 1:1 as the king of the Assyrians, reigning from his capital, Nineveh. Such intentional historical and geographical blunders set the tone of the book of Judith. It accumulates deliberate anachronisms. Not only is Nebuchadnezzar at least six times called "king of the Assyrians," but the fiction reaches the apex of irony when Achior, an Ammonite officer in the "Assyrian" army, recites to Holofernes, the general in chief, Israel's history down to the *postexilic* period. He does not mention Nebuchadnezzar by name, but all the same he describes his destruction of the Jerusalem Temple in 586 and its rebuilding in 515, while the story of Judith allegedly occurs *before* the capture of Jerusalem (Judith 5)! In addition, Nebuchadnezzar is credited here with the capture of the capital of Media, Ecbatana (Jud. 1:14), a feat that historically happened one-half century later, under the Persian Cyrus in 550 B.C.E.

The general in chief of the Assyrian army in the story is Holofernes; he is accompanied by a lieutenant named Bagoas (Jud. 2:4; 12:11). Those names are indeed historical, but they are Persian, not Assyrian or Babylonian. Both men took part in the campaign against Egypt under the Persian king Artaxerxes III in 341 B.C.E.[1] In Judith, Holofernes is at the head of a huge army,

1. Cf. Diod. Sic. xvi.47, xvii.6, xxi.9.

which he moves the incredible distance of 300 miles in three days (2:21). No less taxing to credibility is Holofernes' demand for exclusive worship of Nebuchadnezzar (3:8), for, historically, no Mesopotamian or Persian king was deified. Such a claim was first made by successors of Alexander the Great, two centuries later.

Another anachronism in Judith is the description of Judaea under the leadership of the high priest Joakim (4:6), a situation first encountered under Jonathan, brother of Judas Maccabee, in 153 B.C.E. (cf. 1 Macc. 10:20).

All these inaccuracies, and many others in the book of Judith, are too patent and gross to be unintentional, at least in large part. I said earlier that they set the tone of the story. They definitely put the reader in the terrain of fiction, not of historical report; moreover, they stress its highly ironic character, a deliberate choice of the author, as we shall see later.

The story of Judith clearly consists of two parts of almost equal length. Chapters 1–7 constitute what many critics have considered a protracted introduction to the story proper. Here the Assyrian Holofernes wins the surrender and allegiance of innumerable countries and cities. Their sanctuaries are destroyed by the Assyrian and they are to worship Nebuchadnezzar as the only god on earth. On his way to Jerusalem, Holofernes arrives at the little Palestinian city of Bethulia, an unknown place, allegedly facing Dothan in Samaria.[2] There the situation, not surprisingly, is very tense, especially as the Assyrians have cut the water supply to Bethulia. Under the pressure of the population, the council of elders, at the moment when Judith is introduced in chapter 8, has decided to resist another five days to give more time for God to intervene. After that delay, the city will surrender. But Judith, a pious widow, scolds the elders for their lack of faith. She takes upon herself to do what needs to be done. She goes into the camp of the enemy and makes the Assyrian general lose his head over her beauty, before she beheads him for good. Deprived of their leader, the Assyrians are like a decapitated chicken. A great many of them are massacred by the Bethulians, who celebrate Judith as

2. Surprisingly, E. Bickerman, in *The Jews,* accepts this alleged information at face value. He writes, "Bethulia, somewhere at the edge of the plain of Esdraelon, at a greater distance from Jerusalem than from Tyre" (35; cf. 154).

their savior. She lives to the age of 105 and never remarries, despite having many suitors.

The story reaches its climax in Part II; here the focus is on the character of Judith. Simply to bypass chapters 1–7 as a lengthy and clumsy preface to the story, however, is a mistake. Modern commentators react against such misunderstanding. As writes Toni Craven, "Chiastic structures, thematic repetitions, and corresponding literary features appear in each half of the book. On formal literary grounds, the final text of Judith is both balanced and proportioned."[3] Craven also says,

> The experience of the story is harder if we agonize with the Israelites over the threat of the approaching enemy . . . and come with them to the brink of apostasy. . . . To avoid Part I of the book of Judith is to miss the opportunity to learn what the people of Bethulia seemingly have learned about their God and about proper worship by the end of chapter 16. In the end they have a triumphant song of praise to sing, but this comes only after considerable struggle.[4]

As far as we are concerned here, space does not allow us to do justice to Part I. Our topic is Judith, not an exegesis of the book that bears her name. But Part I cannot be ignored, if only for the reason that I gave earlier: it sets the ironic mood of the whole story. Irony, says Carey A. Moore, is "the key of the book."[5] We have seen how paradoxical it is that Nebuchadnezzar is introduced as king of the Assyrians. It is as if someone were to start a story by speaking of "Napoleon, king of the Prussians, who in 1914 arrived with his troops at the gates of Tiranna, Albania, to besiege it. There he, or one of his generals, was mastered by a woman who abused him, while he planned to abuse her."

The heroine, we are told, keeps a remarkable poise, mindful of all the minutest details, until she cuts off Holofernes' head. In contrast, a seasoned warrior by the name of Achior faints when he sees the severed head that she carries. Particularly striking in the story of Judith are her discourses to Holofernes. They are

3. Toni Craven, "Artistry and Faith," 93.
4. Ibid., 113.
5. C. A. Moore, *Judith,* 78.

literally filled with double entendres. This is exactly what irony is all about. In irony, according to Luis Alonso-Schökel,

> a character says something more or something other than a second character can understand, sharing the irony with the narrator and reader. . . . The "secret communion" or collusion of author and reader at the expense of some character is essential in each case.[6]

The more ridiculous the victim—or, to use the Greek term, the *alazon*— appears, the more we feel it is justified that he is flouted by the *eiron,* the one who uses irony. Holofernes is monstrously vain; he is so conceited that he gulps any flattery. He has locked himself inside of a code from which everything but his ego is foreign. His process of decoding discourse sifts out all that is not himself. Judith does not have to exert herself in the effort to invent a snare for Holofernes. He is so stupidly narcissistic that he loses the game before he starts playing. He is no match for Judith, whose wisdom is praised by people who know what they are speaking about (see 8:29).

Speaking of play and game is perhaps the most appropriate way to dispel the self-righteous condemnation of those who feel that Judith should not have deceived Holofernes and then decapitated him. Of course, to be invited to praise a murderous gyp as a heroine is somewhat embarrassing in religious milieus. But perhaps we need to learn again how to play. In the story of Judith, the men of the establishment keep their hands clean, but the eventual price for their purity is the surrender of Bethulia to Holofernes. The result is that if they reject the redeeming game of Judith, they will have to dance with tambourines to the tune of the Assyrians, as says Jud. 3:7. The next verse says clearly what that tune is:

> He demolished all the sanctuaries [of the vanquished] and cut down their sacred groves, for he [Holofernes] had been commissioned to destroy all the gods of the land, so that Nebuchadnezzar alone should be worshipped by every nation and invoked as a god by people of every tribe and tongue.

Israel's obedience to God's law cannot become an excuse for going back to Egyptian slavery. Judith, after all, by going to

---

6. L. Alonso-Schökel, "Narrative Structures in the Book of Judith," 8.

Holofernes and the Assyrian camp, risks perhaps even more than her own head—she risks her soul. But she saves her people and the honor of God. We shall return to this point.

The book is an anthology of texts about, and allusions to, other women in the Bible: Miriam, Deborah, Jael, Sarah, Rebekah, Rachel, Tamar, Naomi, Ruth, and Abigail, among others. Parallels with Esther and Susanna also are clear. In fact, the cumulative effect is striking; it amounts to a panegyric of the biblical woman. It would be difficult to trace back those allusions exhaustively, but it is worth our while to emphasize a few of them.

Judith is a rich widow (8:7). In Hebrew culture, those two terms are put in tension. On the one hand, her wealth indicates that she is an independent woman and that she is a capable manager, like the wise woman praised in Proverbs 31. She is her husband's wealth, and she makes her household rich by her skill. Susanna provides a parallel here, and Naomi a contrast. On the other hand, Judith is widowed; thus she belongs to the category of those that she herself claims are close to God—the poor, humble, weak, desperate, hopeless (9:11), that is, those who need protection, especially divine protection.[7] Her widowhood recalls other famous widows in the Bible: Abigail (1 Sam. 25:39,42), Bathsheba (2 Sam. 11:26-27), and Ruth. All of these did remarry, and therefore there must be good reasons why Judith chose not to (on this, see below). But, most importantly, all these widows are related to David. The accumulation in the Judith story of lies, deceits, double entendres, assassinations, as well as the beauty of the woman, make one think not only of the episode of the rape of Dinah by the Shechemites in Genesis 34, but also of the triangle David–Bathsheba–Uriah in 2 Samuel 11. As to the beheading of Holofernes, the parallel with 1 Sam. 17:51, David drawing Goliath's own sword to decapitate him, is striking. As Judith brings back Holofernes' head to Bethulia and dedicates to God what she had taken from the general's tent, so had David done with the head of Goliath and the weapons that he brought "to Jerusalem," meaning that he dedicated the Philistine trophy to God. In more than one way, Judith is David in the feminine.

---

7. God is "the protector of widows," Ps. 68:5; Sir. 35:15. The widow represents the suffering Israel, Isa. 54:4, Lam. 1:1, 5:3ff.

Judith also claims to belong to the tribe of Simeon, and this feature is important in the story. Her appeal to "the God of my forefather Simeon" (9:2) accords with a series of late texts that rehabilitate Simeon and Levi after their slaughter of Shechem related in Genesis 34. As is well known, both are heavily criticized by Jacob for that crime. But Testament of Levi 6–7, Jubilees 30, as well as Judith 5:16, 6:15, exonerate Simeon and Levi for having deceived the Shechemites and massacred them when they were lying in bed after being circumcised. Simeon thus is credited for having avenged his sister Dinah by deceit and murder, and that is exactly how his descendant Judith deals later with Holofernes. The bloody story in Genesis 34 is reinterpreted in favor of the murderers because, in the words of J. C. Dancy, "as the Shechemites *polluted* Dinah, so the Assyrians *have planned . . . to pollute* the temple of Jerusalem. As Dinah was a *virgin,* so Judith is a *widow*—each of them weak women."[8] There is here, however, a sort of conflation of the father and sons of Genesis 34, for Judith combines the audaciousness of Simeon with the legendary cunning of Jacob.

Be that as it may, Judith a woman and a widow, without husband or brother—in contrast to Dinah—decides to accomplish her mission, like the heroine in the contemporary book of Esther, through the exercise of "feminine wiles" (cf. Esth. 5:1-8, 7:1-10). Chapter 9, for example, is sprinkled with mentions of femininity and weakness, even and especially with the mention in verse 10 of the Greek term *theleia,* "female," which is applicable as well to animals (also in 13:15 and 16:5; this latter text, by the way, is of particular interest, for it shows with what other pole the author wanted to contrast the term "female"). In 16:6 the opposition is to the "champion" (of the Assyrians), a term used of Goliath in 1 Sam. 17:4, 51. The parallel is all the more striking as Goliath in the Greek Samuel text (v. 4) is called *anēr tunatos,* "the male champion." The Philistine "macho" was killed without glory, but how much more so, if we take Abimelech's word for it, when the warrior is killed by a female! Judges 9:52-54 tells us about the woman of Thebez who broke Abimelech's skull with a

---

8. J. C. Dancy, ed., *The Shorter Books of the Apocrypha,* 103.

millstone. Abimelech then ordered his armor bearer to finish him off, "that people say not of me, 'A woman slew him.'"

Such, however, was the fate of Sisera at the hand of Jael in Judges 5. The parallel with Judith is arresting. Jael also beguiles a general; she also wins his trust in order better to destroy him; the scene also occurs in a tent, and if Sisera is not beheaded by Jael, his head is all the same transfixed by a peg. Furthermore, Jael is eulogized, like Naomi (cf. Judg. 5:24; Ruth 4:14), "blessed among women is Jael," while to Judith it is said almost similarly, "more blessed are you by God Most High than all other women on earth" (13:18). About Judith, as about Jael, the text concludes that she brought her people peace for a long time after that (16:25); in the case of Jael, Judg. 5:31 speaks of forty years of tranquility.

The affinities with Ruth, another widow, are both on the level of particulars and general. It is clear that Jud. 11:23 and 15:12, for example, echo the book of Ruth. In the former text, Holofernes says to Judith, "Your god shall be my god" (cf. Ruth 1:16). In the latter, "all the women of Israel flock to see Judith and sing her praises" (cf. Ruth 4:14f.). But, we must go into more depth. The very name *Judith* means "Jewess." Ruth, by contrast, is a Moabitess. But, in an earlier text, Judith was the name of the Hittite wife of Esau (Gen. 26:34); and the masculine form of the name belongs to a foreigner in Jer. 36:14.[9] The distance, therefore, between Ruth the Moabitess and Judith the Jewess is mediated by the exotic connotations of the latter's name.

This bridging of Judith with Ruth is strengthened in the book of Judith by several details; Judith, for example, lies at the feet of Holofernes (12:15-16), as Ruth had lain at the feet of Boaz (3:7-8). In the final song of triumph that women sing in praise of Judith, they mention her sandal—"Her sandal entranced his eye" (16:9)—reminding one of the role played by the sandal in the Ruth story (4:7ff.). All in all, the parallel between the two heroines is a close one. It is thus not without surprise that we see Judith taking a very different route from Ruth's in purposely

9. At least in the Masoretic Text, where perhaps an original *we-eth* was deleted before Shemaiah, who then is the one said to be "ben Kushi," son of the Ethiopian.

perpetuating her widowhood. As we might expect, the church fathers were impressed with Judith's self-imposed celibacy. For rather different reasons, so also are modern feminists. Among the latter, Patricia Montley deserves special mention.[10] Judith, she says, is the archetypal androgyne, a combination of the soldier and the seductress, or rather, an alternating of "masculinity" and "femininity." In Bethulia, "she plays the man." In Holofernes' camp, she successively plays the woman, then the man in cutting off the general's head. The man's role is extended to her return to Bethulia and until V-day. Then, she reverts to the asexuality of widowhood. Montley writes, "Judith embodies yet somehow transcends the male/female dichotomy."

True, the ideal of chastity is indicative of the date of composition of Judith. Qumran and the New Testament are not far away. The eighty-four-year-old prophetess Anna in Luke 2:36ff. is approvingly described as remaining a widow after spending only seven years with her husband. But, in the book of Judith, one cannot but think that chastity is also a sign of independence. She is without protector, as we saw above, but she does not need any. Her androgyny, as Montley says, is self-sufficient. Something is happening with Judith that announces a new era. The numerous literary parallels established by the author of the story with so many other Bible women are not just for the sake of comparison. The book grants to them en bloc a heretofore unrealized power through the cumulative effect of synchronism.

What brought a second-century B.C.E. author to such a resolve? A good lead to answer this question is again the irony that pervades the book. Irony is not just a literary device to keep up the interest of the reader. It is rather at the service of a work that is polemical and even subversive. In the preceding chapter of this book, we saw that Susanna was not a feminist pamphlet. More than the vindication of (a) woman, the tale centered on the vindication of innocence/justice. Judith, by contrast, is more woman-oriented. Incidentally, it is paradoxical in this respect that Susanna conceivably was written by a woman; but Judith is more

10. P. Montley, "Judith in the Fine Arts: The Appeal of the Archetypal Androgyne," 40.

problematic. The story is told from a male point of view, and this is the reason Toni Craven, in her book on Judith, writes that the story is "thoroughly male dominated."[11] We are thus facing the alternatives of attributing the authorship to a woman purposely adopting a male world view, or to a man subversively magnifying the feminine element in the *Heilsgeschichte*. The situation is thus paradoxical, but deserves to be celebrated. The best advocates for a cause are those who are not self-serving.

In short, it seems that Judith goes one step further than Susanna in its protest. Susanna was subversive by bringing up the case of the justice of a woman flouted by the lechery and hypocrisy of elders. Judith is subversive by showing that a woman can take the lead and become the model of faith and martyrdom, while "elders" recoil in the holes of their complacency. Judith is not only a David redivivus of sorts, she is Judas Maccabee in the feminine; her very name says as much (cf. 1 Macc. 3:1-9). At the time of the composition of Judith, it was surely not a trivial feat to feminize the hero of the day![12]

As in the episode of Deborah, who was flanked by Barak (Judges 4–5), Judith also has a male counterpart in her story. But, although a star in the tale, he is largely outshined by Judith, as Barak was outshined by Deborah. The figure of Achior fulfills here the same function as the oft-repeated mention in the book of Ruth that the heroine is a foreigner. Ruth was of Moab; Achior is of Ammon—precisely the two offspring of the incestuous union of Lot and his daughters (Gen. 19:36-38). Moab and Ammon are "forever" cursed and to be kept out of Israel's community, according to Deut. 23:2-9, restated by Ezra 9:1-2,12, and Neh. 9:2; 13:1-3, as fitted the exclusivism and the defensiveness of the party in power in Jerusalem. To such isolationism the party of

---

11. T. Craven, "Artistry and Faith," 87.

12. For instance, there is an evident parallel between, on the one hand, the beheading of Holofernes and the ensuing celebration at Bethulia, and, on the other, the beheading of Nicanor by Judas Maccabee and the celebration in Jerusalem (1 Macc. 7:47; 2 Macc. 15:30-35). Another possible model directs attention toward the same historical and literary context. Indeed, a parallel is provided by the Maccabean patriarch Mattathias, who showed his zeal for the law and slaughtered the apostate Israelite and the Syrian officer who tried to coerce him to sacrifice to idols (1 Macc. 2:24-26).

opposition, to which the author of Judith belonged, responded with the expressed conviction that the much-expected restoration would not be realized before all nations are involved in the celebration of the "eschaton" with the Jews. And this hoped-for breakthrough entailed for the present community the cancellation of Deuteronomy 23. Thus, Third Isaiah proclaims,

> Let not the alien that has joined himself to the Lord say, "The Lord will surely separate me from his people"; neither let the eunuch say, "Behold, I am a dry tree." . . . For my house shall be called a house of prayer for all peoples.   (Isa. 56:3, 7)

At the basis of the stories of Ruth and Jonah lies the same principle.

The name Achior is perhaps a creation of the author for the sake of drawing a contrasted parallel with Joshua 7. There, to recall, Achan (in the Greek, *Achar*) is summoned by Joshua after the violation of "the devoted thing" *(herem)*. Joshua condemns Achan/Achar to be stoned to death in the valley of *Achor!* Similarly, Achior is summoned by Judith (although not to pass judgment on him). For Achior is the only one in the story who shares with Judith the conviction that the Jews of Bethulia (or elsewhere) are not vulnerable to the enemy as long as their own sins do not render them so. Clearly, such a stance coming from a non-Jew constitutes a foil for the empty religiosity of Bethulia's leaders and populace. Achior, a just man although an Ammonite, stands head and shoulders above the Bethulians. Only Judith casts a taller shadow. He is the anti-Achar who was stoned to death in the valley of Achor for unrighteousness, although he belonged to the tribe of Judah. Achior makes one think of the Mesopotamian prophet Balaam in the book of Numbers, who also delivered oracles of weal about Israel; but Achior goes much further than his model, as his convictions amount to full belief in God; his formal conversion to Judaism in Jud. 14:10 comes as no surprise.

This conversion, by the way, is probably one more ground why the book of Judith was not canonized by the Rabbis. They were indeed much embarrassed by the admission of an Ammonite into the community of Israel, in contradiction to the law. Their occasional justifications of the fact are confused and unconvincing.[13] Modern judgments coming from orthodox Jewish scholars do not, it seems to me, fare any better. For Harry Orlinsky, for example, the main reason Judith was not canonized is that there is no mention in it of Achior being baptized when he converted, a ritual stressed by the Pharisees.[14] In fact, Judith's subversiveness did not escape the Rabbis' notice. The book runs against the stream of "orthodox" Judaism. As Alonso-Schökel writes, Deut. 23:4 "is here intentionally abolished, and with it the policy of Nehemiah."[15] The character of Achior is meant to break up a stalemate and to make an opening on the redemption of some at least among the nations, even though the nations are coalesced against Israel under the leadership of Holofernes. This is a message essential to the opposition party in the second century B.C.E., as we have noted. In contrast to the triumphalism of a conservative party that turned in on itself in an effort to gather strength and to avoid contamination from the impure, the "utopians" saw the withdrawal as a block on the way of history. Their ideal was rather the figure of the Isaianic servant, and this explains why they would have a contender who seems to be weakness incarnate. Judith is a woman, a widow, a loner; in short, she is representative of the *anawim* (the humble, the poor in spirit). She even becomes an alien in her own country as she goes to Holofernes' camp, a plight that Achior shares with her, as he also is an alien in Bethulia.

By contrast, the leaders and the populace of Bethulia are ready to compromise with the Hellenizers. They are characterized by their saying (7:27), "We will be slaves, but our lives will be saved," thus contradicting the Exodus experience. As a desirable woman, alone in hostile territory, Judith could be not only an

13. Cf. *Yebam.* 76b (but see 8:3!); *Yad.* 4:4. In these talmudic texts allowance is made re *female* Ammonites and Moabites, because Deut. 13:9 "speaks of sons, not of daughters"! In *Yad.* 4:4 Judah, Ammonite proselyte, is given permission to enter the Community *(qahal)* on a confused and confusing basis of biblical interpretation.

14. H. M. Orlinsky, *Essays in Biblical Culture and Biblical Translation,* 281. For a contrary opinion, see Shaye J. D. Cohen, *From the Maccabees to the Mishnah,* 53.

15. Alonso-Schökel, "Narrative Structures," 16.

alien but a wanton, for the situation is strikingly similar to the one described figuratively by the prophets. They depicted Israel tempted by the nations, like a lecherous female surrounded by lovers. But it is rather the collaborationists *in* Jerusalem (or Bethulia) that fill that definition, for they compromise with Hellenism and, among other things, become lax on dietary laws (11:12f.). Paradoxically, Judith is *out* of Jerusalem (Bethulia), but she turns the situation around, refusing even there to share with Holofernes the delicacies of his cuisine.

When all these details are taken in consideration, the balance of the narrative comes into full relief. It was necessary to show Judith bereaved by the loss of her husband, for she is a virtuous lady. But she had to remain within the limits of time that allow her to keep her youth and beauty. She had to be presented as a widow, not a virgin, because her widowhood makes her not only available but mature. Furthermore, her asceticism blunts all suspicions that her "flirtation" with Holofernes for a sacred cause would capsize into full-fledged seduction and lewdness, for, as everyone knows, the spirit is willing but the flesh is weak. Not all subsequent tellers of the Judith story related such a balanced version—just look at what some artists and writers have done with poor Judith. Jean Giraudoux in 1931 made her a courtesan and Holofernes a noble character. A second-century B.C.E. literary composition can indeed be much more progressive and liberating than its twentieth-century interpretation!

Judith vindicates the choice of Achior, and she completes his task. He goes away from Holofernes and thus weakens the general through his departure. She comes to Holofernes and kills him through her wiles. It is a killing in two acts. Interestingly enough, the conquest of Jericho by Joshua had also been a two-act affair. In that instance, a proselyte by the name of Rahab had meted the first blow to Israel's enemy (Joshua 2). Rahab too in the book of Joshua is a secondary character, but an important one. She appears at the beginning of the Jericho story and again at its end, thus providing a neat enclosure (see Josh. 2:1 and 6:25). Similarly, Achior is a bridge that unites both sections of the book of Judith. After his testimony to Holofernes about Israel's invulnerability if they do not sin against God, he is at the end the privileged witness of the identity of the one whom Judith has decapitated.

But if Achior is teaching a lesson to the inhabitants of Bethulia, Judith teaches a lesson to Achior. In fact, there is in Judith a kind of stair-step progression. In a first move, as we saw above, the elders of Bethulia, representing the priestly tradition made even more exclusive by the Chronicler, who is also editor of the books of Ezra and Nehemiah, share a perspective according to which divine justice is retributive. In progress on such a stance, Achior describes to Holofernes Israel's history in putting forth the Deuteronomistic notion of "either win or sin." Holofernes will be incapable of conquering Bethulia if its inhabitants are faithful to their God. But Judith goes a step further. Israel *is* sinless, and the principle of retribution must be revised, for, even sinless, Israel is tested by God, as the ancestors before them—Abraham, Isaac, and Jacob. The patriarchs were surely not punished, for they were righteous (8:25-27). Thus, some manuscripts and versions of Jud. 8:27 read, "God is subjecting us to the ordeal by which he tested their loyalty, not taking vengeance on us." There is therefore an alternative explanation of the present suffering of Bethulia.

The narrative of the heroine Judith raises theological and hermeneutical problems. It cancels out Deuteronomy 23 and its laws ostracizing certain foreigners "for ever." Judith demands that the Deuteronomistic principle of retribution be revised. She disregards Deut. 25:5-10 and its laws on the levirate marriage of a widow without child. Her God is not the god of the Priestly tradition that the Chronicler reinforces. But also, by contrast, she displays a strict fidelity to the commandments that the party of the establishment considers as particularly binding. For example, there is a strong emphasis in the story on the Temple, on purifications, fastings, and prayers. All the same, the salvation of Bethulia is wrought without the help of the Temple; the sacrifices are deemed "insufficient to please" God. The real sacrifice is offered by the one "who fears the Lord" (16:16). Instead of going along with the centripetal movement of the conservatives, Judith's move is centrifugal, a feature that is not without reminiscences of the Jonah story. (In a way, Holofernes' camp into which Judith goes is but the extension of Nineveh, the capital where Nebuchadnezzar reigns, according to the fiction of the book.)

We should also mention the ambiguity of Judith's attitude vis-à-vis the civil and religious authorities. She acknowledges the legitimacy of the leadership of the high priest, of the mayor and the government of Bethulia—but she confronts them and calls them all to accountability (8:11). It appears that she assumes for herself their channels of inspiration and warrants of authority, but she herself "has no guarantee or secret word of confirmation."[16] For God acts through secondary causes, without miracles. Sacrifices are not criticized, but they are not commensurate with God's majesty (16:16). She practices mortifications, fastings, *kasherut;* she keeps the festivals and their eves (as later required by the Rabbis)—but one may wonder, with Toni Craven, whether her scrupulousness goes too far. It "surely pokes fun at stodgy notions of propriety and proper religious behavior. . . . The putting of sackcloth on everything in sight, including the cattle,[17] [or] Judith's pausing to pray before chopping off [Holofernes'] head are acts which satirize standard behavior in such settings."[18]

Although some scholars insist on the Pharisaic character of the book, or at least—with Y. M. Grintz[19]—on its pre-Pharisaic *halakhot* (legal prescriptions), it is strange that there is here no angelology when such numinous interventions would be expected—for example, in the scene in Holofernes' tent. Furthermore, there is no allusion to a resurrection of the dead, another Pharisaic tenet, although Judith comes close to such an affirmation in the final hymn. There she says about the Gentiles that God "will consign their bodies to fire and worms; they will weep and feel pain for ever" (16:17).

The conclusion is that the book of Judith represents a religious position that not only historically precedes the Pharisaic doc-

16. T. Craven, "Artistry and Faith," 94.
17. Another parallel with the story of Jonah (chap. 3).
18. T. Craven, "Artistry and Faith," 115–16.
19. Y. M. Grintz, *The Book of Judith* (Hebrew), 15–55.

trines but is anticipatively different from them. The struggle that the book illustrates is between an ideology of theocratic exclusivism and an anti-establishment utopia displaying a great deal of skepticism about the institution's capabilities in a time of crisis. Judith does not shun rituals and exterior marks of piety, but it is clear that her existential options are determined by faith alone. If we have to characterize her religious stance with one word, it is pietism. At the time of Judith's composition, the pietists were called *Hasidim*.

One of the main Hasidic stances was their opposition to an all-out Hellenization of Judaism. The party in power at Jerusalem, as a matter of fact, did accommodate Hellenistic views and ideals in their "modernized" institutions. It is therefore of particular importance for the student of that period (roughly the second half of the second century b.c.e., right after the persecution of the Jews and Judaism by Antiochus IV Epiphanes) to trace Hellenistic characters that paradoxically influenced the book of Judith.[20] For the story is not merely popular literature; it displays features of the Greek romance, a literary genre that flourished during the Hellenistic time.[21] It is characterized by its main ingredients: love and journey/quest or military prowess. It also ends happily after dramatic reversals of fortune, the villain being routed by the hero, and the heroine vindicated in her chastity. The plot uses pathos, often heavily. The romance is intended to stir in us basic emotions of fear, sympathy, and relief. One way to achieve this is by letting the characters of the drama profusely express their own emotions. (This led Hellenistic authors to the innovation of intermingling verse and prose.) When the characters are expressing emotional outbursts, they tend to versify. As Moses Hadas has noted, the mixture of verse and prose had no precedent in classical Greek literature, but the phenomenon is normal in Semitic literature.[22] We are little surprised when Judith "strikes

20. This is a particularity that nearly all anti-Hellenistic literature shares with Judith. One thinks of late wisdom literature or even apocalypses. For a summarizing synopsis of the reception and/or repudiation of Hellenism in Palestinian Judaism, see Martin Hengel, *Judaism and Hellenism*, 1:247ff.

21. We already encountered Greek romance in the chapter on Susanna, above. Julius Africanus (third century c.e.), to recall, had drawn that parallel.

22. M. Hadas, *Hellenistic Culture: Fusion and Diffusion*, 111.

up [a] hymn of praise and thanksgiving, in which all the people join lustily" (16:1).

Sometimes minute details in the Judith story are revealing. Not only does the heroine here choose chastity over remarriage, a feature quite striking by its unusual nature in a Jewish tale, but she is accompanied by a maid who is more of a confidante. Such a character is common in both Greek tragedy and comedy. The maid is often the only trusted and trusting companion of the heroine. In comedy, that representative of the commoners became increasingly important because of the growing democratization of the audience's tastes, until the confidante outwitted and outdid her mistress. It is not irrelevant that the story of Judith ends with the notation that Judith "gave her maid her liberty" (16:23).

Another such detail is the description of revelries in Jud. 3:7 and 15:12ff. In both places, there is a question of garlands used by the dancers. The terms are "crowns" and "thyrses." These are characteristic of the Hellenistic period. In the intertestamental literature one again finds mention of those Dionysos-related ornaments in Wis. Sol. 2:8 and 2 Macc. 10:7.

We cannot leave Judith without emphasizing its ties with Greek tragedy. J. C. Dancy, a British commentator on the book of Judith,[23] calls attention to several points in that respect. As is well known, Jewish tales generally leave little room for direct discourse. They concentrate on the characters' actions and behaviors. There is no Demosthenes in Hebrew literature. But in Judith, direct speech occupies some two-thirds of Part II of the book. Second, although irony is far from being foreign to biblical stories, the use by Judith of tragic irony—whereby, for instance, characters say things that are bound to be understood one (wrong) way by other characters, and another (right) way by the audience—is closer to a Greek model than to a Hebrew one. Third, Judith herself acts as a Greek tragic heroine. According to the classic structure of popular tales, as we saw earlier, there are three main characters: the hero, the villain, the heroine. But Judith is so heroic that she plays the roles of both the heroine and the hero. No other personage in the Hebrew and Jewish literature comes close to such a personal epic. We have seen, furthermore,

23. J. C. Dancy, *Shorter Books of the Apocrypha.*

that Judith's maid takes on more precise contours than most female servants in the Bible, with the exception of Hagar in the book of Genesis.[24] Finally, the rhetoric of certain sentences in Judith's discourse appears as if it came straight from the amphitheater (cf. 8:23; 9:3; 16:7).

Thus, Judith is one example among many of literature belonging to the polemic, subversive reaction of Jewish faithful against the Hellenization process of their society. The story, however, evidences the deep influence of Hellenistic thinking and world view on all layers of Jewish society. There is nothing surprising in this. Each epoch faces new problems and is stirred by new provocations of all sorts. Each has to invent a new language adapted to the new problematic. But the present-day use of a vocabulary drawn from semiotics or deconstructionism, for instance, does not mean that one necessarily approves of such methods. Judith is the product of its time. If there were no Hellenistic influence on the story, its message would be insular and irrelevant, a timeless abstraction. My last point now will show how deeply Jewish and, by contrast, how little Greek the tale of Judith is.

We have seen above that in talking with the elders of Bethulia, Judith straightforwardly deals with the question of suffering, suggesting on that occasion another interpretation than the one of retributive justice. The patriarchs also, she says, were tested by God, not punished for sins they did not commit (8:25-27). But Judith goes further. She invites the inhabitants of Bethulia to offer themselves in oblation for the sake of Jerusalem (8:21-24; 13:20). Moreover, it is what she personally does immediately after her exhortation to the leaders. She adorns herself as a sacrificial victim. From now on the enemy's attention will be forced upon her instead of on the whole of Bethulia. She makes of herself a substitutive offering. As Craven writes, "Judith's great beauty invites assault."[25] In other words, it is so true that "deliverance is decided apart from the priesthood and the numinous presence of the Jerusalem Temple"[26] that the "altar" is symbolically translated into Holofernes' tent.

24. Hagar, however, does not stand out as servant, but as Abraham's mate and Ishmael's mother.

25. T. Craven, "Artistry and Faith," 86.

26. Ibid., 94.

It is to be stressed here that the idea of substitution, invented or re-created by Second Isaiah (or his disciples), was treasured by the party of opposition in Jerusalem after the "restoration." Of particular interest here is the much-debated text of Zechariah 12. Second Zechariah as a whole sequentially reviews the four songs of the Servant of YHWH.[27] Zechariah 9:9-10 parallels Isa. 42:1ff.; Zech. 11:4ff. parallels Isa. 49:1ff.; Zech. 12:10—13:1 corresponds to the third Song (Isa. 50:4ff.); Zech. 13:7-9, to the fourth (Isa. 52:13—53:12).[28]

Along the same line of tradition, Judith substitutes herself, as a propitiatory sacrifice, to an establishment that has lost its head, much before Holofernes loses his for other reasons. When those in charge of the public protection are disheartened and thus expose their protégés, these must either undergo slaughter or take their fate in their own hands—thus, perhaps, saving themselves *and* their appointed leaders. How they do that may take different forms. According to Isaiah and Zechariah, the Servant goes through substitutive suffering and death, and God only can change his failure into victory, his death into life. The book of Judith, influenced as it is by a Hellenistic world view, stresses instead heroic substitution, and Judith's victory is not post-mortem, although it is in extremis. In both cases, the results are comparable and the premises similar. Of the two, Judith is perhaps to us more understandable and imitable than is the Suffering Servant—but, ultimately, Judith saves only Bethulia, whereas the Servant of YHWH redeems the world.

27. See my study of Second Zechariah, particularly on Zech. 12:10ff. in "Aggée, Zacharie, Malachie," CAT 11C.

28. This background is necessary for an understanding of the message of Zech. 12:10, *"et aspicient ad me quem confixerunt"* (they shall look upon me whom they pierced), for the phrase is a commentary, or a midrash, on the Suffering Servant and an eschatologization of that figure. In his vision of the End, the prophet, expressing his feelings about the profound rift that had yawned between an arrogant party in power in Jerusalem, on the one hand, and the disenfranchised Judaeans, on the other, builds on the base laid down by the figure of the Servant of the Lord. The "just" goes through martyrdom, and his suffering is at least in part inflicted by the "establishment." Judah is martyred by Jerusalem, the party of utopia by the party of ideology. At the eschaton, the "burghers" of Jerusalem "pierce" the "provincials" of Judah, and realize too late their crime against none else but God, who identifies himself with his Servant. Their repentance transforms the martyr's failure into victory and his death into life.

CHAPTER 5

Esther

In a way, our next heroine is more difficult to introduce. The problem is not that the book of Esther is less interesting or less vividly written, however. Were our topic the so-called Jewish question, for example, no other document of the Bible would provide more arresting terms and more provocative perspectives. Our problem is the character of Esther, while the author's emphasis, as C. A. Moore says rightly, is "on plot and action, not character or personality." In fact, he adds, "[the] major characters are . . . superficially drawn."[1] The author's skill is displayed entirely in the story he tells, and especially in his masterful use of irony. Already on this score the parallel with Judith is striking. Beside the tongue-in-cheek utterances of King Ahasuerus/Xerxes and, for instance, his ridiculous edict that man is master in his house (1:22), Esther goes from transgression to transgression of the royal orders and is rewarded in the process (5:1f.,8), while Vashti is summarily deposed after one act of disobedience (1:17-19). Speaking of obedience, Haman must comply with a very humiliating royal order that makes him honor a man he planned to hang (6:11f.), but Mordecai is rewarded after disobeying a royal command (3:2; 8:1f.). Such deftness in the use of irony at times raises the style to a powerfully suggestive level. For example, we find in 3:15 a telling contrast between tyrants and popu-

1. C. A. Moore, *Esther,* AB 7B, LIII. Robert Alter as well speaks of Esther's characters as "schematically conceived." The book, he says, is "a kind of fairytale . . . richly embellished with satiric invention [and] comic art" (*Art of Biblical Narrative,* 34).

49

lace: "Then the king and Haman sat down to drink, but the city of Susa was bewildered." Later on, Haman, mistakenly thinking it is himself that the king wants to honor, goes far overboard in suggesting what should be granted to such a man. It is then disclosed that the king had Mordecai in mind, and that Haman is to help glorify him (6:6-9). We finally reach the apex of irony when the plot as a whole ends with a sting: Haman is hanged on the same gallows that he had erected for Mordecai!" (7:10).

Irony is also built into the structure, the remarkable balance of which has been demonstrated, in particular by Sandra B. Berg.[2] The author repeatedly uses the root *gdl* (great) to emphasize the comic paradox of Haman elevated (becoming great) by action of the king, until he is "elevated," physically this time, on the gallows that he erected for Mordecai (7:9-10). The latter meanwhile goes from menace, torment, and humiliation to a veritable elevation. Concerning Haman, there are numerous illustrations of his climbing the social ladder (see 3:1; 5:11); then the text shifts focus and all the occurrences of the root *gdl* apply to Mordecai. (In 8:15, he receives a high diadem; then his progressive promotions are punctuated with the adjective "great" in 9:4 [twice]; 10:2 [twice]; 10:3.) The promotion of Haman by the king had been paradoxical in the first place. Immediately after the description in 2:21-23 of how Mordecai's loyalty saved the king's life, the following verse abruptly reports the promotion, not of the faithful, but of Haman. Such crisscrossing situations delicately indicate that Haman's glory is usurpation, while Mordecai's is justice.

The king orders Mordecai and everyone else to kneel before Haman. Mordecai refuses, not through bitterness, but because he is a Jew—at least this is the reason invoked somewhat cryptically by the text (3:4). Later, it becomes clear that Mordecai has been in firm control of the situation from the beginning. He had recommended to his niece, who is also his adopted daughter, not to reveal her Jewish origins; now he challenges Haman's authority. Both elements, secrecy and civil disobedience, belong indeed to a master plan that consists of risking an enormous wager—namely,

---

2. S. B. Berg, *The Book of Esther: Motifs, Themes and Structure.*

the very lives of the Diaspora Jews, including Esther and himself—in order triumphantly to overcome the enemy. (The literary success of such plots was demonstrated in a modern film, *The Sting,* whose title would fit the book of Esther as well.) Bruce Jones is correct to deplore the negative response that Esther has elicited from liberated women. Such a misunderstanding stems from missing the humorous nature of the tale. There is indeed here an accumulation of grotesque excesses. Vashti is treated as a sex object to be displayed or summarily discarded when she refuses to comply with an outrageous demand that she play the star of a burlesque. At that point, says Jones, the king's "seven wise princes . . . escalate Vashti's modesty into an imperial crisis."[3] Ahasuerus interrupts his drinking bout to issue an edict that throughout his vast empire the husband will be master at home by royal fiat (1:22). The whole episode serves the interests of Esther, and, behind her, of Mordecai. But the selection of the new queen is the occasion of another pastiche. The pleasure of the king is paramount. The new "Miss Persia" must be beautiful and virgin. Esther is described as having a beautiful figure (2:7). That is all that the king is after (2:9). We then learn that the candidates go through a yearlong beauty treatment before they are offered to the royal lust. After the wedding night, the woman is sent to a second harem where she may well stay without ever being called again by the king, unless he remembers her; the text more crudely says, "unless the king desired her" (2:14).

What is described here does not belong simply to a cold description of ancient mores. Rather we are presented with a satire. Elias Bickerman writes, "The despot who delivers a people to his vizier without even knowing its name, is the same who before puts away his wife by caprice and, then, executes his vizier on the word of Esther."[4] As a rabbi said, Ahasuerus is the one "who sacrificed his wife to a friend, and then his friend to his wife."[5]

To be sure, the tale's caricature of the Persian court rests on a partial truth. What is stressed by the magnifying glass of irony is

---

3. B. W. Jones, "Two Misconceptions about the Book of Esther," 175.
4. E. Bickerman, "Notes on the Greek Book of Esther," 124.
5. Quoted by E. Bickerman, *Four Strange Books of the Bible,* 205.

the discrepancy between the pitiful insignificance of the king's personality and the immense power of decision of his words. Not surprisingly, the author of Daniel, around the same epoch, describes this terrifying paradox by using the image of a monstrous animal (or a horn on its head) uttering "enormous things" (Dan. 7:8). The fool is speaking and the crowd is awestruck, construing the sound and fury as ironclad law.

In fact, in order fully to savor the tale, it is important to understand the legal backdrop against which it unwinds. "In the political theology of the Persian kings,"[6] the king himself *is* the law. His person and the unlimited legal power it represents is, in fact, the only decisive factor of cohesion in his immense and motley empire. That is why the king's will is equated with truth and righteousness, the attributes of the god Ahura Mazda. Therefore, by definition all insubordination is lie and injustice.[7] Biblical texts of that time show how Jews were deeply impressed with such a conception of law that was so foreign to them. Both Daniel (6:9,13) and Esther (1:19; 8:8) mention with amazement the irrevocability of "the statutes of Persia and Media."[8] The biblical authors use the Persian loanword *dat,* which in Hebrew came also to mean "religion." The Persian kings were no gods by nature, but there was little difference between royal and divine will—so much so that the king's unlimited power smothers itself and enslaves the lawgiver. The king is unable to cancel his own decision either to throw his friend Daniel to the lions or to allow the massacre of a whole population (Dan. 6:15-17; Esth. 8:8; see Diod. Sic. XVII:30).

Let me say in passing that the Iranian understanding of law made a strong impact upon Jews and Judaism. When, in the aftermath of the first waves of returnees to Zion, the governors

6. Ibid., 191.
7. A refinement of this idea in some modern empires involves equating any dissidence from the regime with mental illness.
8. The irrevocability of Persian law is confirmed by Diod. Sic. (see, e.g., book XVII:30. The text reports the case of a man put to death under Darius III (336–330) even though he had been shown to be perfectly innocent. "[Darius III] immediately repented and blamed himself for having committed such a great error, but it was impossible to have undone what had been done by royal authority."

Ezra and Nehemiah are appointed by the Persian king in the fifth century, their mission is clearly defined. They come to Jerusalem to give to Torah the authority of a state law, something the "law of Moses" had never been before. As the Persian law is *dat* endowed with divine force, so Torah became a divine hypostasis of sorts, a status it never lost since in Judaism.

This interpretation of law found its dramatic application at the time of Alexander the Great and the Hellenization of the East. Alexander was moved by a philosophical dream of unifying the world into a single home for all people, an *oikoumēnē*. All particularities had to be transcended by universal realization of a supreme principle, a supreme *nomos* (law). The challenge to the Hellenistic age was to discover that golden fleece. There were many candidates for legal universality. Jews also proposed their Torah given by the living God on Mount Sinai as the world *nomos*.

But these avatars of the Persian royal edicts take us beyond the epoch of Esther. The endeavor of Haman—"the enemy of the Jews," as he is repeatedly called—receives, however, all its meaning from that context. He describes to the king an anonymous unruly people, whose laws are not the king's dictates. In such cases, Persian kings often had recourse to transplantation of entire populations. But the people in question is already scattered; so, urges Haman, the only solution is the "final" one. They must be "destroyed, slain, and annihilated, all of them, young and old, children and women, in a single day . . . and their possessions plundered" (Esth. 3:13). To make the proposition more acceptable to the king, who might worry about the loss of so many taxpayers, Haman offers to pay 10,000 talents of silver to the state treasury; that is, it has been estimated, some two-thirds of the annual income of the Persian empire (cf. Herodotus 3.95, "the yearly tribute to Darius amounts to 14,560 talents."). Josephus noted that the sum proposed by Haman was the estimated price for the Jews had they been sold as slaves.

This, by the way, makes us better understand Esther's argument with the king in 7:4. She tells him, "we have been sold, me and my people, to be destroyed, slain and annihilated. And even if we had been sold into slavery, males and females, I would have said nothing about the fact that such an onslaught *[hazzar]* would not compensate *[showeh be]* the damage made to the king." The argument is purely economical. As writes David Daube, the book means to demonstrate "that a government has more to gain by orderly taxation than by giving over the Jews to massacre."[9]

But Ahasuerus/Xerxes seems not to understand that lesson at first. Making the Jews outlaws excludes them from the empire and, certainly, from royal protection. They become nonentities, nonexistent. Even before they are physically exterminated, they are without rights of any kind.[10] They may be abused and plundered with impunity.

Ironically, those accused by Haman of being unruly are in fact disobeying unjust, ungrounded, or outright ludicrous laws, such as bowing before an egomaniac courtesan, or risking one's head in appearing before the king when not officially summoned. By contrast, the Jews are also those who save the king's life, while others pretend to be law-abiding but either plot against the king or dream of substituting their own power for his (chap. 6). Implicit, of course, is the idea that the laws the Jews observe, and that Haman describes with an astounding superficiality as "different from every other people's" (3:8), might be better than those enforced at the Persian court.[11]

Be that as it may, the book, albeit without express mention of the Torah or, for that matter, of anything religious, including God—a point I shall emphasize below—is the story of the clash between two laws and, beyond that, between two world views. One could also define the problem as a contest between two inviolabilities. The denouement of the story will show that what is inviolable is the Jewish people, not an abstraction such as the

9. D. Daube, "The Last Chapter of Esther," 140. The author defends the authenticity of Esther 10. The loss incurred by the king in cancelling the pogrom was compensated through a legitimate tax, probably on Mordecai's proposal.

10. Some modern regimes dismiss all opposition as "hooliganism."

11. Haman's accusation against the Jews was a common one in the Hellenistic world. Josephus reports it in several of his writings, see *Ant.* 4.6.8 (137) or *Apion* 2.7 (79). Tacitus and other Roman historians later sharpened their criticism and accused the Jews of being misanthropes (see Tac. *Hist.* 5.5, among other texts).

"Persian law" (6:13; cf. 4:14). When ideology prevails over humanity, the machine indiscriminately crushes friends and foes. It belongs again to satire to show that the first victim of legal inflexibility in the story is neither a Jew nor an outlaw. Summoned by her godlike husband to appear at the royal banquet at Susa, Queen Vashti refuses and is summarily put aside.

Ancient and modern interpreters have been puzzled by the attitude of Vashti. It was understood already by the Rabbis that she was to appear naked at the banquet. Being under the influence, the king was boasting of all his riches and possessions. What better example of ownership could he display than the queen's beauty itself? Persian custom may have been for wives to leave the banquet before the drinking bout. At that point, concubines came in.[12] Thus, the king deals with Vashti as with a courtesan, and she has little choice but to decline. Her refusal, however, raises a grave legal problem. As the king is personified law, he has a very narrow margin of choice. He sets an example, which he confirms by decree, and ironically degrades Vashti to the status of concubine, which she tried to avoid in the first place. So the fateful circle of tragedy locks upon itself, allegedly for the sake of law and order.

The paradox is that tragedy gives rise to comedy. With Vashti's humiliation starts the story of salvation, a story worthy of the full attention of modern liberation theologians. Vashti's demotion is Esther's promotion. The book of Esther is fond of those reversals of fortune that strike parity between Jews and their neighbors or enemies and eventually reveal the Jewish appointed destiny. This principle of peripety, the Aristotelian *peripeteia* (sudden change of fortune),[13] is in Esther a veritable although implicit theology. That is, the story is entirely constructed upon the unpredictability of history, so that, in the ironclad determinism of causes and effects, or of Persian law, one must always consider the possibility (or should we say the faith?) of deliverance coming

---

12. So it seems according to Dan. 5:2,3. It is contradicted by Herodotus 5.18 and Plutarch *Artaxerxes 5*. On Persians' notorious predilection for liquor, see Herod. 1.133.

13. Aristotle, *Poetics* 1452a, 24–26.

"from some other place" (4:14, *mi-maqom aher*). As Esth. 9:22 expresses it so pointedly, "the opposite happened" *(nehpakh lahem)* from what was planned by the oppressor.[14] It is now time to deal with some features that are repeated in almost all the introductions to and commentaries on Esther, but which are necessary to mention here for our purpose. Ostensibly set in the days of Xerxes I (the fifth century), the story, whatever its remote origins, was composed during the second century in the eastern Jewish Diaspora. Its geographical cradle is pointed to by an accumulation of "Persianisms" in the story. Furthermore, the names of the characters take us to the region of the Tigris. Already in the 1890s Heinrich Zimmern and Peter Jensen equated Mordecai and Esther with Marduk and Ishtar, and Haman and Vashti with the Elamite gods Humman and Mashti. These German scholars concluded that the story of Esther was a historicized myth or ritual.[15] In 1950, Theodor H. Gaster suggested that the prototype of Purim is the Persian new-year festival, and he saw in Esther "simply a Jewish adaptation of a popular Persian novella"[16] (more on this point below).

A most intriguing theory has been put forward by Robert Gordis. In a 1981 article entitled "Religion, Wisdom and History in the Book of Esther—A New Solution to an Ancient Crux," the Jewish scholar insists on the uniqueness of Esther in the Bible, since it purports to be composed "in the form of a chronicle of the Persian court, written by a Gentile scribe." Such a literary device was used by the author to "buttress [Jewish] confidence in the veracity of his narrative."[17] Gordis recalls the famous case of the Letter of Aristeas, which is allegedly written by a non-Jew as an apology for the Jews.

I do not accept Gordis' theory as it is, but it is crystal-clear that the tale of Esther is perfectly suited to a Diaspora milieu. Not

14. Also when the Persian king decides something, "the opposite happens"! *(we-nahaphokh hu, 9:1)*.

15. P. Jensen: "Elamitische Eigennamen. Ein Beitrag zur Erklärung der elamitischen Inschriften." H. Zimmern, "Zur Frage nach dem Ursprung des Purimfestes."

16. T. H. Gaster, *Purim and Hanukkah in Custom and Tradition,* 35.

17. R. Gordis, "Religion, Wisdom and History in the Book of Esther,—A New Solution to an Ancient Crux," 375.

only is the story set in the Persian court and not only are the Jewish characters Jews of the Dispersion, but the literary genre of the tale is what German critics have felicitously called *Diasporanovelle*. What makes this expression difficult to render in English is that the *novelle* is an oft-cultivated genre in the German language but not as much in the English.[18] It is a short story but with developments through peripeties that make the plot rebound toward an unexpected denouement. One example of this in the Bible is the story of Joseph (Genesis 37–50)—which, by the way, is also a *Diasporanovelle*.[19] Esther displays extraordinary characteristics that Gillis Gerleman calls "a consciously consequent

---

18. W. Lee Humphreys mentions Herman Melville, *Billy Budd;* Henry James, *The Turn of the Screw;* Joseph Conrad, *Heart of Darkness;* John Steinbeck, *The Pearl.* See George W. Coates, ed., *Saga, Legend, Tale, Novella, Fable: Narrative Form in Old Testament Literature,* 82ff.

19. Particularly illuminating is the following summary written by E. K. Bennett on the nature of the *novelle:*

> The Novelle is an epic form and as such deals with events rather than actions; it restricts itself to a single event (or situation or conflict), laying the stress primarily upon the event and showing the effect of this event upon a person or group of persons; by its concentration upon a single event it tends to present it as chance ("Zufall") and it is its function to reveal that what is apparently chance, and may appear as such to the person concerned, is in reality fate. Thus the attitude of mind to the universe which it may be said to represent is an irrationalistic one. It must present some aspect of life (event, situation, conflict) which arouses interest by its strangeness, remoteness from everyday happenings, but at the same time its action must take place in the world of reality and not that of pure imagination. It depends for its effectiveness and its power to convince upon the severity and artistry of its form. Characteristic of its construction is a certain turning point, at which the development of the narrative moves unexpectedly in a different direction from that which was anticipated, and arrives at a conclusion which surprises, but at the same time satisfies logically. It should deal with some definite and striking subject which marks it clearly and distinguishes it from every other Novelle. This striking element in the subject matter is frequently connected with a concrete object, which may in some Novellen acquire certain inner symbolical significance. The effect of the impact of the event upon the person or group of persons is to reveal qualities which were latent and may have been unsuspectedly present in them, the event being used as the acid which separates and reveals the various qualities in the person or persons under investigation.
>
> By its very objectivity as a literary form it enables the poet to present subjective and lyrical moods indirectly and symbolically. It concerns itself with a small group of persons only, restricting itself to those who are immediately connected with the problem or situation with which it deals. Its origin and home are in a cultured society.

desacralisation and de-theologisation of a central salvation history tradition." Gerleman thinks here of Exodus/Passover.[20] He writes, "The history of Esther and of Purim is from the outset presented and shaped as in contradistinction with the story of Exodus and Passover."[21] Arndt Meinhold is surely right in rejecting Gerleman's theory,[22] but the latter is not without a residue of truth inasmuch as it was simply an exaggerated conclusion from an uncontrovertible premise. So, for example, Haman defiantly casts lots on the thirteenth of Nisan, immediately before Passover, which falls on the fourteenth–fifteenth of Nisan, that is, the first month of the year. The cast lots designate the thirteenth of the last month, Adar, for the fateful massacre of the Jews, just one month before the following Passover, but in all this the Jewish celebration is not mentioned. That strange absence is not accidental. Does it point to a Diaspora rejection of the old festival and its replacement by Purim, as Gerleman believes? It is more likely that Esther's silence about Passover is to be put on the same level with Mordecai's order to Esther not to reveal her Jewish origins. As we saw, even God is not mentioned; nor is a Jewish festival of any kind. There is neither allusion nor reference to the land of Israel—a fact that remains without parallel in the Bible and the Apocrypha.[23] Salvation for the Jewish community comes from the Jews themselves, not from any transcendent intervention, miracle, or deus ex machina. Furthermore, as Meinhold has astutely pointed out, while the Exodus tradition involves the leaving behind of the foreign land, Esther's concern is precisely to stay there! Jews may occupy high positions, even at the royal court, and become queen or vizier, prime minister or governor, but for them the issue always remains one of survival. Passover and the exodus are assuredly not forgotten at Susa, but a stronger imperative for Persian Jews is to find a modus vivendi with their non-Jewish compatriots while keeping their identity as

20. G. Gerleman, *Esther, A History of the German Novelle,* 18–19 esp. 11, 14, et passim.
21. G. Gerleman, "Studien zu Esther: Stoff-Struktur-Stil-Sinn," 28; *Esther,* 23.
22. A. Meinhold, "Die Gattung der Josephsgeschichte und des Estherbuches: Diasporanovelle II."
23. Bickerman, *Four Strange Books,* 198.

Jews. To a certain extent, their singularity makes them strangers in a strange land. As Mordecai makes clear to his niece, the queen, her ascension (that is, Jewish assimilation) is not the goal but only a beginning (of a development that may indeed lead either to death or to a Jewish presence in Persia without loss of identity).[24]

From that perspective, it is politically expedient that Esther keep her Jewish origins secret, while Mordecai is almost without exception called "the Jew." Another view, however, is Henri Cazelles' suggestion that the book of Esther is the outcome of the mixing of two originally independent sources that we shall here call E for Esther and M for Mordecai. E has a rather liturgical character and is at home in the Persian province. M is political and is located in the capital Susa. It celebrates the victory over Haman ben Hamdatha and his sons. Moreover, throughout the book there is a series of doublets that corresponds to the juxtaposition of E and M. In Esther 9, for example, there are two massacres, one on 13 Adar (source M) and another on 14 Adar (source E); verse 18 collapses both into one. There are two narratives of the death of the ten sons of Haman in chapter 9 (vv. 10 and 13) and two decrees about Purim, one by Mordecai (v. 23), the other by Esther (vv. 29ff.; v. 31 harmonizes).[25]

The hypothesis is appealing but seems unwarranted. The duality of themes corresponds to an almost perfect symmetry between the two parts of the story, a pattern strongly emphasized by Sandra Berg,[26] and from which Joyce G. Baldwin infers the story's unity, based on role reversal (from triumph to defeat, or from elevation to downfall in the case of Vashti, Haman, and the Jews' enemies; from humiliation to victory in the case of Esther, Mordecai, and the Jewish community).[27]

The heroine's name is double, corresponding to the fact that the whole story is built by pairs. Hadassah, her Jewish name, however, is barely mentioned. Her official civil name, Esther, is the name by which she is known by her contemporaries and by

24. See A. Meinhold, "Die Gattung," 78.
25. H. Cazelles, "Note sur la composition du rouleau d'Esther," 17f.
26. Berg, *Esther*, passim.
27. J. G. Baldwin, *Esther*, 28.

tradition. Daniel and his companions likewise have dual names, but the balance is tipped the other way in the book of Daniel. The accent there is definitely on the keeping of Jewish identity in a potentially adverse foreign situation, indeed in a situation that had become, at the time of the book's composition, full-fledged persecution of the Jews. In the book of Esther the tale is concerned to show the face of the Jew that is turned toward the world. Figuratively speaking, Esther at the "synagogue" is Hadassah. But the tale bypasses this aspect of her life. She is envisaged from start to finish at the royal court of Ahasuerus, where she is known as Esther. The other face remains more or less hidden, sometimes concealed and sometimes revealed. Not that there is a split in Esther's personality, but in a Diaspora situation it is the "Esther" aspect that gives substance to the "Hadassah" aspect. "Who knows," says Mordecai at the hinge point of the story, "if it is not for a time like this that you reached royalty?" (see 4:14). It is indeed one important aim of the story to display the conflicting loyalties of the Jews in Diaspora. Mordecai refuses to prostrate himself before Haman—but not through rebellion, for he had already proved his loyalty toward the king (2:19-23). Esther disobeys the king (4:11), but it is ultimately for the good of the state (7:4). There is thus an ethical, or religious, or ethnic allegiance that supersedes all others, but whose outcome is a better service to the king than that which is rendered by those who claim to have a singular allegiance. As Baldwin writes, "Civil disobedience of a minor nature is seen to be justified in a greater cause, namely, the genuine good of the state (7:4)."[28] Such an argument has been picked up by Jews and Christians until this very day. Its potency depends upon the premise that God's will does not run contrary to the *veritable* interest of the *res publica* (the state) but, on the contrary, God knows best what is good "for the king." When the latter realizes this, he elevates Joseph, or Daniel, or Esther/Mordecai, to the highest position in the empire. Meanwhile, however, the danger is great and it is lethal, because the king is easily misled by court intrigues and power games. Then the Jew is falsely accused of disobedience, of partic-

28. Ibid.

ularism, of arrogant contempt, and other such crimes. But, scape-goating him is often meant to better hide the turpitude of the real culprits.

The *Diasporanovelle,* be it the story of Joseph, or of Daniel, Judith, or Esther, describes a tense situation for the Jews in a foreign land. They must bear two names and two faces, have two calendars and two agendas, don two sets of clothing, eat at two tables, hold two discourses, live at the edge of two worlds. Not so much in spite of this as because of it, they become prime minis-ters, princes, or queens. Their Jewishness raises them above the mediocrity of soothsayers, above the morbid narcissism of cruel viziers. The option of serving God first eventuates in an option for the state, for the world. Esther saves not only her people; she saves the Persian Empire from being doomed by Hitler-like Haman the Amalekite. That is why, in the book of Esther we read the surprising note that the inhabitants of Susa rejoiced with the Jews at the "enthronement" of Mordecai (8:15) and that many even became Jews (8:17).

It is also the Diaspora condition that explains the allusive nature of Esther's theology. A parallel has often been drawn with the Joseph story in Genesis. The similarities between the two tales are ideological and even verbal.[29] On the religious level, there is in the Joseph story a kind of eclipse of the divine. André Neher has called attention to the absence of divine discourse in the narration from Genesis 37:1 to 46:2.[30] Neher has correctly pointed out that the setting of the Joseph story in Egypt renders improper the direct involvement of God. The theophanic dia-logue with the covenantal people occurs only in the land of Israel. On a foreign soil the contact is only indirect, through dreams for instance, and through coincidental or serendipitous events.

The Joseph story, however, is theocentric. The history of salva-tion is God's business, and such ultimate causality is clearly

29. See in particular L. A. Rosenthal, "Die Josephsgeschichte, mit den Büchern Esther und Daniel verglichen." Also, S. Niditch, *Underdogs and Tricksters,* chapter 5. The Jewish Midrash draws numerous parallels between the two stories—some of them, one must say, less convincing than others. See Louis Ginsberg, *The Legends of the Jews,* vol. II "Joseph."
30. A. Neher, *The Exile of the Word: From the Silence of the Bible to the Silence of Auschwitz,* 24ff., "The Silence of Providence: Joseph."

indicated in the texts (cf. Gen. 39:2-3,21,23ff.). The author of Esther goes further. He avoids *any* mention of or even allusion to the Deity in the Persian setting. In other words, there is a theology for the land of Israel and another for the Dispersion; or, more accurately, there is a language for those within "Erez Israel" and another language for those without. This is all the more understandable as the problems are highly different according to their settings. Esther's problem is Jewish survival under the threat of genocide. To that problem the book gives an answer inspired, not by the possible model of the exodus from Egypt under the leadership of Moses, but by the one of the safe management of Egyptian affairs by Joseph, who stayed in the foreign land and made his people *and* the Egyptians prosper. The Joseph model, however, did not go far enough in "detheologizing" its language. Part of the reason is perhaps the kind of danger in Joseph's story. It is a natural disaster that threatens Joseph, the Hebrews, and the foreigners together. As such, it is not sufficiently typical of Diaspora problems, which are of a historical sort and threaten to deeply divide Jews and non-Jews into hostile camps. In Esther the danger of Jewish annihilation issues from the setting itself. The foreigners are dangerously ambivalent, their attitude ambiguous. One day they may command that all Jews in the empire be massacred, and the next day elevate one of them to quasi-kingship, promise half of the empire to another Jew because she is attractive or sexy, and side with those they first selected for annihilation.

Joseph was endowed with a wisdom far above the average. He had premonitory dreams, revelatory visions, an unflagging certainty of his high destiny. Such is not the typical plight of Diaspora Jews. Some of their own may occupy envied positions of power—at times, for no better cause than that they are handsome. But the fact is that they hold their destiny in their own hands. Their survival is somehow a certainty that history has upheld, but not by supernatural means. Mordecai says to Esther that if she is unwilling to act on behalf of her people, help will come from another place, but that other place is certainly no deus ex machina. Put in a nutshell, the "theology" of the book of Esther is Judeo-centered. Human action—*Jewish* action—either assists or resists the ultimate causality beneath the surface of events. When there is conformity between the two, history appears as a serendipitous sequence of cause and effect. At the end, no other alternative is left to the Jews but to celebrate and let their joy explode with thanksgiving.

Once more we note that this document represents a stance that cannot be reconciled with Ezra-Nehemiah's efforts to protect Jewish identity from contamination with foreigners. From the point of view expressed in the Chronicler's literature, the restoration announced by the prophets would occur at Zion, no other possible setting; among the returnees from exile and not among others; in the revived cultic celebration in the temple of Jerusalem and not in the occurrence of any particular historical event. From that perspective, it is clear that Esther constitutes an uphill *apologia* for Diaspora Jews. Here, the Jews of Susa are bona fide members of the elect people of God. They are entitled to institute a festival of their own, a far-reaching decision running counter to Palestinian "canonical" rigidity. When we turn to some observations about Purim, the contrast between homeland and Diaspora will appear in even greater relief.

Esther shows no concern or interest for the temple and the cultic activity in Jerusalem. There is no attempt to get advice, much less approval, from Judaean authorities. The Diaspora community appears in Esther as self-contained and independent. S. D. Goitein goes so far as to suggest that the recurring banquets in the book of Esther are the Diaspora equivalent of the Palestinian "land flowing with milk and honey."[31]

Although Purim falls exactly one month before Passover, no parallel between the two festivals is drawn by the story itself. It is evident that for the Diaspora Jews, the commemoration during Passover of the return of the land stirred a weaker response. The content of Purim is a far cry from that of Passover.

As David Clines says, the message here is

> a reassurance to diaspora Jewry that collaboration with the authorities is no sin against Jewish identity. For it is possible for Mordecai *the Jew* to stand next in rank to the King, *and* at the same time to be

---

31. S. D. Goitein, *Iyunim ba-Mikra,* 59.

popular with his coreligionists (10:3). The story has given the lie to Haman's initial charge that "it is not for the King's profit to tolerate" the Jews (3:8).[32]

Purim is not the raison d'être of Esther's story. With Ernst Würthwein, one must distinguish between the genre *(Diaspora-novelle)* and its use as an etiology of Purim *(Gebrauchsgattung, that is, the subgenre of festival-legend).*[33] As a story, the *novelle* of Esther precedes the Purim-legend. But, in the absolute, Purim was a preexistent foreign festival. It is today clear that the Hebrew loanword *Purim* comes from Old Assyrian *puru-um* and *purum,* according to the title of an epoch-making article by J. Lewy.[34] The word *puru* means "lot," secondarily "fate." It is, however, probably a mistake to focus attention on the singular form *pur* given in Esth. 3:7 and 9:24, and then to see in *purim* a plural. This gives way to an abstraction foreign to the intent of the text: *purim* would recall the double fate decreed for the Jews by Haman and by God (see the verb *haphakh* in 9:1,22, "the reverse happened"). *Purim* is rather, I believe, a Hebrew transliteration of the Assyrian *purum,* and has originally no plural connotation. But, because the Hebrew refers to casting "a lot" (and not "lots") and because there is in the tale a striking symmetry of its parts, *Purim* was divided, so to speak, into two parts or two *pur,* a linguistically hybrid creature. Ideologically, however, this artificial creation proved a very effective Hebraization of a foreign vocable, and *of a foreign festival.* It seems established, as a matter of fact, that the "lot" in question refers to the reversal of destinies marked by the New Year casting of lots in Babylon in the last moth of the year (Adar). What the Babylonians celebrated in that most important season of the year, the veritable acme of their religious life, had its proper *hieros logos* (legend or myth). The book of Esther provides a Jewish legend to replace the much older Babylonian or Persian ritual, thus transforming it

---

32. D. J. A. Clines, "Ezra, Nehemiah, Esther," *The New Century Bible Commentary,* 262.

33. E. Würthwein, "Esther," in *Die fünf Megilloth,* 170ff. The subgenre in its turn reacts upon the primary genre and imposes some of its laws (cf. P and the Pentateuch), in this sense E. L. Greenstein's thesis (see n. 36 below) is correct.

34. J. Lewy, "Old Assyrian puru'um and purum"; A. Ungnad, "Eponymen," 420, 448.

into a Jewish commemoration. The reversal of winter into spring and of the destinies of gods and humans by the casting of lots now leaves room for an accumulation of historical coincidences, to the point, it is true, that they become implausibilities.

One night, says Esther 6, the king had insomnia and had someone read to him. The document that was taken from the shelves happened to be the annals of the empire, the best soporiphic of the time. The "book" was opened at random and the passage read to the king happened to be the one about Mordecai's revelation to the king of a plot against him. The wicked Haman also happened to be wide awake that night and, despite the incongruity of the hour, came to speak with the king of his plans to hang Mordecai. The king gave him audience, but rather than listen to what Haman had to say, the king began to ask him how best to honor someone the king felt indebted to. Haman, assuming that he was the one the king was speaking about, answered accordingly, suggesting fantastic honors. When he realized that the king was in fact speaking of Haman's enemy Mordecai, it was too late to recant his words. Adding insult to injury, the king happened to choose Haman to implement his own fantasies at Mordecai's benefit. The story goes on along that line, with other "miraculous" or at least felicitous reversals of bad luck for the Diaspora Jews. Here also, therefore—but definitely on a historical rather than cosmological level, as in Babylonia or Persia—Purim celebrates the passage from death to life. The old mythological demons of Chaos in the Babylonian ritual have been replaced by historical anti-Semites with Haman at their head, on the model of Tiamat, or, more fittingly, Kingu. As Abraham D. Cohen writes,

> Purim which, to the nemesis of the Jew and to an alien system of thought, affirmed the operation of chance and fate in the universe, becomes, for the Jew, the anti-chance symbol, the symbol of that which God so readily controls to *His* ends.[35]

The Judaization through historicization, or, put negatively, through "demythologization," is still more pointed when we follow the lead of the tale and realize that the story is not without a

35. A. D. Cohen, "Hu Ha-Goral: The Religious Significance of Esther," 94.

religious historical-traditional background. In fact the stage set of Esther is the unfinished business reported in 1 Samuel 15.[36] There, we are told that King Saul spared the Amalekite Agag and plundered the Amalekite property, instead of fulfilling the divine command of killing the former and putting the latter under "ban" (ḥerem). This became the ground for Saul's rejection as king and the beginning of his fall.

In Esther, Mordecai is introduced in 2:5 as a descendant of "Kish, a Benjaminite," the father of Saul. He refuses to bow before Haman, but this is not a display of arrogance in flagrant violation of the king's orders; instead, Mordecai's refusal is justified in the text by the mention that he is a Jew. The witnesses of Mordecai's insubordination, we are told, were waiting "to see whether Mordecai's words would stand, as he had told them that he was a Jew" (3:4). This statement would remain cryptic, were it not that we happen to learn that Haman is "the son of Hamdatha the Agagite" (3:1), thus a descendant of Agag, the Amalekite king spared by the ancestor of Mordecai! The two archenemies are face to face once more, Saul and Agag, Israel and Amalek.[37] The later development of the tale may well be retrospectively indicative of the reason Mordecai commanded his niece not to reveal her Jewishness. A premature proclamation by Esther of her origins would short-circuit Haman's plans; Mordecai wants Haman to devise his "final solution" to the Jewish problem. For a long while in the story, it seems that Haman disposes of the power of life and death over the Jewish people, but the truth of the matter may be that he is manipulated by his intended victim. Mordecai counts on the hostile and murderous instinct of the Amalekite, knowing that Haman's thirst for Jewish blood will push him to extremes and at some point drive him out into the open where he will be exposed. There Mordecai is waiting with a sling of his own, capable of killing another Goliath.

36. W. McKane, "A Note on Esther IX and I Samuel XV"; E. L. Greenstein, "A Jewish Reading of Esther." The thesis of the latter refreshingly original article is put in a nutshell on p. 233: "How but in jest could a Jewish story name its two heroes after the Babylonian god and goddess Marduk and Ishtar? . . . The scroll was custom-made for the feast [Purim]."
37. The Midrash Esther says that had Saul not spared Amalek, there would have been no Haman! (Introduction 7, p. 2b of the "Horeb" edition, 1924.)

Haman must feel free to vent his rage against the Jews, lest he beget another generation of "Amalekites" that will further torment Israel and try to exterminate its people. That the Jewish fortune was reversed (*nehpakh,* 9:22) and Haman and his nest of serpents was destroyed by Mordecai's scheme deserved to be celebrated "by every single generation" (9:28). For, as the story of Esther demonstrates, Amalek is the symbol of the perennial presence of evil in the world, of the enemy wherever Israel moves.[38] "Mordecai's Jewish identity presents dangers; Esther's Jewish identity resolves them."[39] To be sure, Esther's initial silence for a good cause can easily lead toward Jewish assimilation and loss of identity, especially in a time of crisis. Then, what originally was meant as a tactical maneuver in the hands of providence amounts to betrayal of the community for the sake of selfish interests. Mordecai warns Esther against this: "If you persist in keeping silent at this very time . . . you and your family will perish" (4:14).

It was befitting the traditional distribution of functions between genders to have male aggressiveness adopted by Mordecai the Jew, and a female secretiveness assumed by Queen Esther. What is highly remarkable, however, is the reversal of roles— among multiple reversals of fortune—between the two. After an initial attitude of subordination vis-à-vis her uncle and adoptive father (2:10,20), Esther abruptly orders him to explain his actions. Mordecai complies but returns his own command to Esther (4:8). Esther sends an additional order to Mordecai (v. 10) and gives him instructions (v. 16). Mordecai, then, "did exactly as Esther had commanded him" (v. 17). In a similar vein, Mordecai lures Haman in the open; and Esther kills him. Mordecai institutes the festival of Purim; and Esther gives the institution its royal confirmation and solemnity.

One recognizes here and elsewhere a similarity of accents in Esther and Judith. In both stories, which were composed in roughly the same period of time, there is a rather long prepara-

---

38. According to D. J. A. Clines, *The Esther Scroll: The Story of the Story,* it may well be that the story of Mordecai and Haman constitutes the original version of the Esther story. See note 25 above.

39. Berg, *Esther,* 82.

tion before the heroine occupies the center stage. In Esther, that
occurs only in 4:4, while Judith is introduced in chapter 8 of that
book. It is also worth noting among *externalia* that, in parallel
with Judith, Esther is the only biblical book not represented at
Qumran. Neither of the two was canonical there. Qumran knew
nothing of a Purim festival. The covenanters most probably were
displeased with the absence of any mention of God in the book,
with the nonrespect of the dietary laws by Esther, and with her
hesitation before helping her people (4:10-14). Furthermore,
Qumran was not the only milieu disputing Esther's canonicity.
We happen to learn about dissenting opinions, down to the third
and fourth centuries c.e., in the talmudic tractates *Megillah* 7a
and *Sanh.* 100a. Among Christians as well, the book of Esther
was very often noncanonical in the eastern churches. It is, after
all, not even alluded to in the New Testament. There was no
Christian commentary on Esther until the ninth century. To
return to Jewish attitudes, the general welcome that the book
received at a certain point of history should not conceal the fact
that for a long time the orthodoxy in Zion resisted its "canonization" and the celebration of Purim as a bona fide Jewish festival.
The very chronological gap between the first Mordecai-centered
version of the story in the fifth or fourth century[40] and its later
versions during the Hellenistic period in Palestine shows how
slowly the idea of a Diaspora contribution to Israel's thinking
became worthy of consideration and ultimately acceptable.

It must be realized that Esther as a *Diasporanovelle* introduces
brand-new elements in the composition of Judaism. This is especially true as, originally, it was not the "tamed" story it became
later by a generalized skipping over of its troublesome features,
some of which we have recounted in connection with Qumran's
neglect of the book. Such a "sanitized" reading goes hand in hand
with early attempts at smoothing the rough angles of the story by
interspersing additions into the text. Those (Greek) additions,
six in number, describe premonitory (prophetic) dreams, prayers
of Mordecai and Esther, declarations by the queen of her loath-

---

40. This first version was midrashic and referred, as 10:2 attests, to the annals
of the kings of Persia and Media.

ing of Persian food and bed, and other such pious trappings that, of course, radically change the nature of the tale.

The Greek versions of Esther, however, began to be composed shortly after the Hebrew text. The textual history of the book seems to be the following. A first version of the Esther story came into existence in the fourth century B.C.E. or during the Persian period. The final version in Hebrew as it is transmitted in the Masoretic Text dates from the Hellenistic period. Since 2 Maccabees knows of Esther and Mordecai—there is here reference to a "Day of Nicanor" at the eve of a "Day of Mordecai" (2 Macc. 15:36; 1 Macc. 7:49)—the terminus ad quem for the Hebrew text of Esther is the turn of the first century B.C.E. Ruth Stiehl puts the date at about 140 B.C.E.[41] As to the Greek text, a colophon indicates a date of composition around 78–77 B.C.E.[42]

At any rate, the Septuagint shows that the story of Esther was soon understood or reinterpreted as conveying a religious message. The allusions to the historic confrontation of Israel and Amalek in the book were readily picked up and amplified—but with a twist. In the Greek of 9:24, as well as in the Addition to 8:12 (= 16:10), Haman is called a *Makedon*. He was "a Macedonian, an alien in fact" who, says v. 14, plotted "to transfer to the Macedonians the sovereignty [now held by] the Persians." On the other hand, the Jews are called by the king, "well disposed toward the Persians" (v. 23).

This tradition proved very popular among the Jews. In the tenth-century Hebrew paraphrase called the *Yosippon*,[43] Haman is "the friend of the Greeks." So are also Bigtan and Teresh, the plotters against the king's life in Esth. 6:2. They all connive to deliver Persia to the Greeks.

One finds other indications in LXX Esther that Haman was a stranger in Persia. In 3:1, 8:3,5; 9:10,24, he is an Agagite (i.e., Amalekite) or, by a possible play on words with Agag, he is a

41. R. Stiehl, "Das Buch Esther."
42. See E. Bickerman, "The Colophon of the Greek Book of Esther," 362; on the Greek text of Esther, see C. A. Moore, *Daniel, Esther, and Jeremiah.*
43. For the *Yosippon,* see Israel Levy, "L'histoire de 'Suzanne et les deux vieillards' dans la littérature juive," 166–71; *Ency. Jud.,* s.v. "Josippon," 10:296–98; *Sepher Yosippon,* ed. David Flusser.

Gogite (i.e., coming from the cursed city of Gog). More puzzling is the variant in Esth. 9:24 in codex Sinaiticus. There Haman is an *Ebugaios,* a term that remains unexplained but is assonant with another term in Additions to Esther 12:6 where Haman is a "Bugaean." Helmer Ringgren thinks of *baga,* epithet of Mithra, thus making of Haman a worshiper of Mithra.[44] In any case, Haman is presented as a spy for the Greeks, a parasite in Persia, a man whose claim of fidelity to the king is a cover-up for his ill intentions. Those he accuses of his own crimes, the Jews, are in reality "loyal Persians." They even save the king's life without being at first rewarded for such a token of their law-abiding dedication to their adopted land.

It is clear that Haman may ostensibly belong to any nation or group that happens to be inimical to the Jews at a given time; that is probably what "Ebugaios" means. "Gogite," on the other hand, is certainly symbolic and goes beyond a mere updating. It eschatologizes the notion. This decisive step was first taken by the Greek translator of Esther. It is the first evidence we have of a well-established tradition that sees the presence of "Amalek" in every generation, until the eschatological "Gogite" is destroyed and the kingdom of God is established. For the Rabbis of old, Amalek is the epitome of evil on earth. It has remained so until today; the commandment to blot out their memory is still read annually in all Jewish congregations on the Sabbath before Purim (see *Sanh.* 20b). Amalek is the last roadblock before the triumph of God according to the Midrash.[45]

The very repetition in the Scriptures of the curse against Amalek (Exod. 17:8-16; Num. 24:7; Deut. 25:17-19; 1 Sam. 15; 1 Chron. 4:42f.) demonstrates that the Midrash is the result of an enduring tradition. We are consequently invited by the Greek text of Esther to read the book as the record of the fulfillment by the Jews of the Persian Diaspora of the commandment against Amalek. If so, the Esther story would report with a remarkable sense of understatement a historic breakthrough in the stalemate

---

44. H. Ringgren, *Esther.*

45. In Midrash Psalms (9:10 on Ps. 9:7) it is said that the name of God and the Throne will be complete only when the remembrance of Amalek has perished. In Exod. 17:16, as a matter of fact, Yhwh is written YH and *kisseh* (throne) *kes.*

of Israel's struggle with evil in the world. The concealed claim of the book would be eschatological.

As R. M. Hals writes in reference to the book of Ruth and to 1 Samuel 17, "A story can be eminently theological in its intent even though the writer himself speaks not at all of God directly, but chooses to let his characters [let us add: or the events themselves] speak for him. . . ."[46]

Esther is a subversive piece of literature. It belongs with other such productions in the Bible that react sharply against the Jerusalem establishment, especially after the reforms of Ezra and Nehemiah in the fifth century. Ruth the Moabitess leaves the periphery and comes to the center; Jonah leaves the center and goes to Nineveh. As for Judith, she does not take us to far-off royal courts, but all the same the distance is not great between such courts and Holofernes' camp. Esther, like Daniel, is far from Jerusalem and demonstrates that the fate of Diaspora Jews *is* the fate of Israel.

In fact, the parallel between Esther and Judith is more far-reaching than indicated above. In both stories, the central issue is Jewish survival in the midst of a fatal danger. The sequence is the same: life threat, deliverance, vengeance, triumph, institution of a commemorative festival. In the background of Judith's story, the author shows the immensity of the Assyrian army, reflection of the huge power of Nebuchadnezzar. In Esther's story, similarly, the background is provided by the unlimited wealth of Ahasuerus. Such displays are a literary device to impress the reader with the enormous odds to be faced by the Jews for their survival. They are properly unsurmountable. The dramatic effect has impact, and the ultimate victory of the weakest over the mightiest is miraculous. As Corneille wrote, "A victory without risk is a triumph without glory." When, against all expectation, the Jews succeed in turning the odds to their advantage, they are said to inherit a great power for themselves, either through booty, as in the book of Judith, or through donning royal vestments and attributes, as in the book of Esther. This dramatic reversal of situation is characteristic of both stories.

It is, moreover, of particular interest that women are here and

46. R. M. Hals, *The Theology of the Book of Ruth*, 4, note 7.

there instrumental in bringing about the reversal. In both cases, the course of history is changed by a daring act of the heroine. Judith and Esther fearlessly penetrate into the very heart of the threatening stronghold and confront the enemy face to face. Their mode of operation is, of course, determined by their gender. They tap all the resources of their femininity. Thus there is indirectness in their approach. Any other strategy would be sheer folly. But if the method is indirect, the aim is straightforward: nothing short of the total removal of the threat by the death of the foe.

The feminine stereotype is left behind, but these women are not transformed into men. They show the way to men without themselves losing their congenital graciousness. Judith appears as infinitely desirable. Esther remains forever Queen Esther, with the pageantry that that title conveys. They perform as "Judges" did in Israel, restoring Hebrew justice by which the rich are humiliated and the wretched glorified. The event is perpetuated through its annual celebration (Judith 16; Esther 9–10), so that the occasion is raised to the status of symbol and paradigm.

However, these women's origins presaged little of their future destinies. True, Judith is a wealthy woman, but she is without helper. She is a widow and apparently has no brother or other kin to lean on. Esther is an adopted child, an orphan, and the Bible constantly puts that status on a par with widowhood. So, both stories tell about the rise of powerless females to a position of power in a strongly male-dominated world.[47] Holofernes is almost a "macho" caricature, and the male dominance at the Persian court is much stressed; there is even a state law ordering that "the wives will show respect to their husbands, from great to small" (1:20) and that the language at home must be that of the man. This is not alien to the complaint expressed by Nehemiah

47. In contrast with Ruth, in Esther the female queen is the public authority, while the male Mordecai is the behind-the-scene power. On that paradigm of authority and power, see M. Weber, *The Theory of Social and Economical Organization.*

According to Jon D. Levenson (private communication), women's power in the Bible is *rhetorical.* It manifests itself by persuasive argumentation in favor of the innocent (so Abigail, Ruth, Esther . . .); or against the innocent, in the case of Sarah or Jezabel. Levenson's insight is interesting; it does not work in the case of Judith, however.

(13:24) that in mixed marriages Jews were speaking their wives' languages rather than the Judaean.

Chances are that Esther's character originally was even more soberly described than the way it appears in the latter versions of the story. We have no way to know for sure. But the present emphasis on the erotic aspect as a means of overcoming the enemy points definitely in the direction of the Hellenistic novel. It makes one think of the "eroticization" of Hebrew narratives by Josephus, Philo, or the Testaments of the Twelve Patriarchs. Of course, Judith is typically a Hellenistic novel;[48] on that score again, Esther and Judith are closely related. It is characteristic of this literary genre, for example, that both strip off their mourning clothes and don queenlike attire. They appear, however, before the powerful male rulers as utterly powerless, throwing themselves at the feet of the men and stirring in them a feeling of dominance that is rapelike.

To the extent that Judith and Esther are associated and even identified with their people, their humiliation and their symbolic violation by the brute beast reflect Israel's predicament. There is in both stories a parabolic movement of descent of the heroines to the abyss of their people's despondency in order to make the people ascend under their leadership to the summits of glory. Perhaps here as in Zech. 12–13 or Daniel 11–12 the figure of the "Servant of the Lord" served as a model.[49]

The parallel between Esther and Judith is made stronger still in the Greek additions to Esther. In 14:2, Esther strips off her royal garments and "puts on the garb of distress and mourning." Then, in 15:1, she adorns herself again. The change of clothes is also a familiar trait of the Judith story. In a similar vein, Esther declares that she is "alone, with no helper but thee" (14:3). In the same chapter, she claims that she did not eat nonkosher food (vv. 17–18). She takes along her two maids, especially one on whom she leans (15:2). She comes to the king "in the height of her beauty" (15:5); and so forth.

The contrasts between the two tales are also important, how-

48. See U. von Wilamowitz-Moellendorff, *Die griechische Literatur des Altertums,* 189; cf. 142.
49. See above chapter on Judith *in fine.*

ever. Esther starts in a state of desperation. She hesitates before interceding with the king for her people. There is, furthermore, a flagrant opposition between, on the one hand, Jud. 15:7,11 insisting upon the looting of the camp of the Assyrians rather than on their massacre, and, on the other, Esth. 9:5ff. delighting in the description of the enemies' slaughter, at the exclusion of plundering their properties (9:10; 10:3). Clearly, in Esther the accent is on legitimate Jewish defense without greed, while in Judith it is on the miraculous shift from death and famine to abundance and riches.

In short, there are some diverging elements between Judith and Esther, but never outright oppositions. Even minor details are common to both. At a banquet, Judith disposes of Holofernes; likewise at a banquet, Esther exposes Haman. Holofernes dies by his own sword; Haman dies on his own gallows. Judith has a convert to Judaism in the person of Achior. Similarly, Esther speaks of conversions en masse (8:17; more subtly, 9:27). Both books display a strong belief in a synergetic relationship between God and people. In Esther, as we know, that theological principle is more implicit than in Judith, but in Esther as well the great wonder is that "the opposite happened" (9:1) from the determined course of history.

It is important, for instance, to realize that in Esther the Jews' restraint from plundering, despite the royal permission to do so, is the belated fulfillment of the divine prohibition to loot Amalek in 1 Samuel 15. From that perspective, certain elements of the *Diasporanovelle* are put in a new light.

Indeed, to many readers the accents of vengeance and bloodthirstiness in the book of Esther are embarrassing. Also the animosity against Amalek so many generations after the events of the Exodus appears to run counter to the biblical virtues of forgiveness and magnanimity. For these and other reasons—especially the book's nonreligious language[50] —Esther is not particularly appreciated by Christians. It often stirs "righteous" protests against the complacency displayed in relating the Jewish mas-

50. Should it not be seen as a great achievement in a time such as ours, which is more and more suspicious of religious jargon?

sacre of 75,000 people in Persia and the hanging of Haman with his ten sons.

Beyond the fact that such negative reaction is the manifestation of a misplaced mercy, as it badly misunderstands what Amalek represents and "flattens" the symbol to the immediacy of the literal, the very plot of Esther is an anticipative reply to humanitarian protests. The "Amalekite" Haman is not killed in cold blood and just because he happens to be "son of Hamdatha the Agagite." Haman's evil dispositions and designs express themselves without provocation. His unjust rage against one individual is so inflated that it becomes genocidal.

It is that blind rage in Haman that allows Esther or her substitute Mordecai to take control of the situation almost from the beginning and progressively to bring the beast to bay. Indeed, the Jewish reading of the story as seen in the Midrashim emphasizes the irony so evident in the tale not only by stressing the corresponding guile of Esther (in chap. 5, for instance), but in amplifying Esther 6 to mean that during the king's insomnia, he realized that Haman was out to kill him as well as Mordecai, his loyal subject. He therefore decided to have Haman honor his archenemy Mordecai.[51] In the same vein, the king affected to be mad at Haman when he saw him bent over the couch where Esther lay.[52] Furthermore, *Megillah* 16a sees irony in the last term of Esth. 6:4, "for him." The context demands that we understand "for Mordecai," but, as indeed Haman will be hanged on the gallows he had prepared, "for him" must mean "for himself"!

Be that as it may, it so happens that, without divine intervention and without prodigy or external hardening of anyone's heart or other such heavenly push or shove,[53] Haman provokes his own destruction. His wife and friends had predicted that much to him (6:13). The story speaks of manipulation, but not by a deus ex machina. Mordecai and Esther display mastery in bringing the enemy to bay, but, by so doing, they do not take advantage of any kind of immunity; it is precisely the main ideological contribu-

---

51. See Rav Shlomo Henoch, *Eben Shoham* (ancient commentary in Hebrew on Esther).
52. Shlomo Halevi, *Midrash Megillath Esther* (sixteenth-century).
53. Cf. Exod. 4:21; 7:3; 10:17; 11:10 (Rom. 9:18).

tion of Esther to put Jews in the presence of an insurmountable obstacle. As I said above, the background is the unlimited wealth and the omnipotence of Ahasuerus, which a Jewess at the risk of her life must neutralize. The dramatic effect is as strong as in folkloric tales of Saint George and the dragon.

When the parallels to salvation history are missed, one is doomed to misunderstand the book of Esther. An example of this is provided by David J. A. Clines, especially with regard to the events of 14–15 Adar. Granted, they are reported with great soberness by the tale and much is left unexpressed. But there is no excuse in positing, as Clines does,[54] that Mordecai's turn of fortune has converted everyone in Persia into a *philo-Semite!* According to that premise, the Jews would have no enemy left to attack them by taking advantage of the license given them by the first royal edict to slaughter the Jews and—an especially luring permission—to plunder their goods and properties. So the plot that started with the development of the motif of self-defense becomes one of the sheer massacre of an unprovoking and peaceful population branded by Jewish intelligence service as Jew-haters or Jew-enemies (Esth. 9:1,5,16)! One must then attribute to the book of Esther feelings of ultranationalism pushed to the extreme of considering the Jews superior to all other human beings.[55]

In fact, if there is in the story a possible discrepancy between part one (the threat) and part two (the deliverance), it is not due to a change in the plot at midcourse, but to the necessities imposed by the parallel, central to the whole story, between the Persian events and the episode of Saul and Agag. As the latter had armies clashing, so here Haman must have an army of his own that Israel defeats as she did under Saul. As the confrontation reported in 1 Samuel 15 was between two kings, so it is necessary that Haman and Mordecai be invested with royal authority. The Persian king gives his signet ring, first to Haman

---

54. Clines here follows the lead of L. B. Paton, *A Critical and Exegetical Commentary on the Book of Esther,* 280: "So completely were the tables turned, that it was now dangerous not to be a Jew." For a contrary opinion, see Moore, *Esther,* 82.

55. See W. McKane, "A Note on Esther IX and 1 Samuel XV."

(3:10), then to Mordecai (8:8). Similarly, after Haman is elevated
to a position of personal representative of the king (3:1-2), Mordecai appears as kingly in 6:8-11 (proleptically) and 8:15 (defini-
tively). Clines's theory of Esther as an evolving story/text condemns him to miss this point. He wonders why Esther "set[s]
Mordecai over the house of Haman" (8:2) and comments, "Nothing comes of it. . . . The sentence in the Masoretic Text is gratu-
itous. . . .[56]

There is certainly no need to imagine that a sick mind produced at this juncture the description of a ganglike slaying of
innocent people solely because they were not Jews. So much of
the reverse has happened in actual history that the very conjuring
of such a reading of Esther is fraught with a suspect attempt at
exonerating anti-Semites by charging the victims of the same
crime in other circumstances. The author of Esther had no need
to disguise any innocent bystander into Jew-hater or Jew-enemy.
Esther 9:15-16 indicates, to the contrary, that there were enough
Persians who tried their luck in slaughtering Jews according to
the terms of the first royal decree. It is those irredentists who are
called "Jew-haters." They were routed by their intended victims,
not because they were peaceful and disarmed, but because the
fear of the Jews (indeed a religious awe) had fallen upon them.
The "miracle" is indicated by such light strokes throughout the
story.

Indeed, the whole scene can be interpreted as wishful thinking
on the part of perennial victims.[57] Esther is a tale, not a historical
record. Wishful thinking is here not only poetic license; it belongs
to the compensatory imagination of the powerless. The oppres-
sed never miss the recourse of imagining the oppressors being
seized by a more or less supernatural fear of the victims or of
what the victims represent, be it innocence or justice or a
divinely appointed destiny. Then, of course, "no one can stand
before them, for the fear of them fell upon all people" (9:2).[58]

56. Clines, *Ezra, Nehemiah, Esther*, 104.
57. See S. Niditch, "Legends of Wise Heroes and Heroines," 450: "It shows
how the downtrodden turn the tables on would-be oppressors—a common
wish-fulfilling message of traditional narrative."
58. Contra Clines, *Ezra, Nehemiah, Esther*, 42.

But wishful thinking does not mean that imagination is given absolutely free rein. In a traditional society, more so than in an uprooted one, collective memory shapes the imaginations. The little Jewess becomes queen of Persia, like the Hebrew slave had become the alter ego of Pharaoh; Mordecai is a descendant of King Saul and Haman a descendant of Agag. So all the characters are set aside for the fulfillment of their respective roles. When the drama eventually unfolds, "Agag" is killed by "Saul,"[59] and history after being long disoriented is reoriented. Each one has received his lot. Everyone has met his destiny. The celebration can begin.

Some critics have stumbled over the point that the Jews of Persia refrained from spoiling the goods of their foes (Esth. 9:10, 15-16). Indeed this statement, repeated in the texts, raises problems. King Ahasuerus had given the Jews permission to plunder (8:11). Furthermore, if the parallel with 1 Samuel 15 holds, the Jewish restraint in the time of Esther seems to be at odds with the divine command to Saul to put the Amalekite property under ban, that is, to destroy it utterly. W. McKane is gravely mistaken, however, when he interprets the Jewish constraint at the time of Esther as disinterest in the concept of the "ban." He also consistently sees the extermination of Haman's house as an "uncomplicated and untheological [motif] of revenge," on the ground that the author of Esther believed in the "intrinsic superiority of the Jews over the Gentiles."[60]

Nothing is further from the truth. First, it must be remembered that for P already, the "ban" no longer results in the destruction of the items dedicated to God (see Lev. 27:21-29; Num. 18:14). Second, a distinction must be made between Haman and his sons, on the one hand, and, on the other hand, those who attacked the Jews in Persia, thus taking advantage of the first royal edict. While Haman is "Amalek," the 75,000 slaughtered by the Jews in defending themselves, according to the allowance of the

59. Agag, to be sure, was slain by Samuel (1 Sam. 15:33), but several Jewish sources say that Agag had time to beget a child.

60. Clines, *The Esther Scroll,* 261, sees in the Jewish restraint a sign of "the weakness of the plot's conception." The same critic, however, is right to state that there is a "downplay of the 'victory' idea" in the fact that the text qualifies the festival days of "rest."

second royal edict, are not. They are Persians. To mark that distinction, Haman is called by an Elamite name (see above) and the LXX, as we noted, calls him a "Macedonian."

Third, it is clear that the royal permission to plunder ran counter to the divine commandment to Saul in 1 Samuel 15. In Esther's time the Jews did not repeat the sin of their forebears. They would not even touch their enemies' property (Esth. 9:10,15-16). For the enemies' goods are of two provenances— they are Haman's (Agag's), and they are Persian. The plunder of either one was not recommended. Indeed, it was much wiser to let the spoils go to the royal treasuries (so Rashi, Ibn Ezra, and others). Greed, we may recall, had been an incentive for Ahasuerus' earlier edict (see Esth. 3:9) and for Saul's blunder centuries earlier. It was expedient to demonstrate to the king that he did not lose any income by rescinding the effects of his first edict, which allowed the massacre of the Jews in his empire (see 7:4),[61] and to demonstrate to all concerned that they had no mercenary interest,[62] in contrast with those who attacked them. Although permitted by the king to enjoy the spoils, the Jews renounced them, a gesture that would belong to the world of anecdote if we had not the background of 1 Samuel 15.

Finally, McKane has overlooked a crucial point. First Samuel 15 reports events that occurred in Palestine. Esther 9 translates the reader to Persia, to the Jewish Diaspora in Susa. The "ban" in Saul's time was ordered for spoils of war with Amalek. In Persia the property of the Jews' enemies is no spoil of war and is not even "Amalekite." As to the royal allowance, it intended the taking of spoil, not its annihilation in a "ban." A separate case, of course, are Haman's house and goods. But if Mordecai had the desire to destroy Haman's former assets, he was not at liberty to do so. The only way to fulfill the spirit of 1 Samuel 15 at Susa was to turn the affair as the book of Esther did: the king gave Haman's property to Esther (8:1,7)—and who is the fool who would destroy the royal present? Esther was not a fool. She put Morde-

---

61. This is at the basis of Haman's offer to compensate the king for the loss incurred if the Jews are exterminated and their properties looted (Esth. 3:9).

62. Rav Valerio, *Yad Hammelekh* on Esth. 9:15 (sixteenth century, quoted by *The Megillah,* 123).

cai, the descendant of Saul, in charge of the estate of Haman the Agagite (see 8:2). The verisimilitude of the tale demanded that conclusion.

Nothing is more unfair—but also unfortunately more common—than to misrepresent the episode under consideration as "evidence of a kind of diabolical purity of motive"[63] (read: evidence of Pharisaic duplicity and hypocrisy); for those Susa Jews had scruples at plundering properties, but none at massacring 75,000 people! Conveniently, one feigns to forget that the slaughter ostensibly occurred in self-defense and as the sequel of an intended "final solution" to the Jewish problem in Persia.[64] Along that line, M. Fox suggests that 8:13 be translated "to deliver themselves from their enemies." "N q m designates the exercise of legitimate power outside a judicial context."[65]

Thus the story of Esther presents us with a Diaspora interpretation of Scriptures adapted to new circumstances and new conditions. It is in rudiments the kind of hermeneutics that more and more prevailed in a Judaism deprived of land, state, temple, institutions, ministerial officers, and so forth. A *Diasporanovelle*, the book of Esther was the harbinger of an astonishingly adaptive Judaism that lasts until this very day. It is therefore of the highest interest to situate the book of Esther in a hermeneutical trajectory connecting the hoariest past with the ultimate future.[66] The story of Esther starts, in fact, with Gen. 36:12, 16; Amalek is born from the impure union of Esau (the one hated by God, Mal. 1:2)

63. McKane, "A Note on Esther," 261, marks his agreement with M. Haller, *Esther,* and H. Ringgren, *Esther.* Already Martin Luther wrote that the Jews "love the Book of Esther which so befits their bloodthirsty, vengeful, murderous greed and hope." See H. Bornkamm, *Luther and the Old Testament,* 188–89.

64. The Jewish victory in Susa is equivalent to a successful insurrection in the World War II–era Warsaw ghetto with the result of 75,000 S.S. troops being slaughtered!

65. M. Fox, "The Structure of the Book of Esther," 295, n. 9.

66. The book of Esther has been traditionally read with that trajectory in mind by the Synagogue. *Esther Rabba* affirms that when the Messiah will come, Purim will still be celebrated. The book is thus proleptically read in the light of the future. It is also read in the perspective of the past. In the fourth century the Amora Rava stated that at Mount Horeb the Torah was forced upon Israel, who had no choice but to accept its yoke. In Esth. 9:27, however, Israel freely and joyfully took upon themselves, indeed they "confirmed what they had already accepted" (*b. Shabb.* 88a).

with his concubine Timna (whose name means "forbidden"), sister of Lotan the Hurrite (i.e., a Canaanite; his name means perhaps "cleavage"). So Amalek becomes "the prime of nations," but "its future is ruin forever," says Balaam (Num. 24:20). Not surprisingly, the descendants of Esau's historic blunder mount a vicious attack from behind against the children of Jacob in the desert, at Rephidim (Exod. 17:8-16; Deut. 25:18-19). Then YHWH promises to blot out the memory of Amalek, and Moses comments, "As a hand was raised against the throne of the Lord, YHWH is at war with Amalek from generation to generation (Exod. 17:16).[67]

When the time comes for God to liquidate that obstacle on the road to history fulfillment, he orders Saul to exterminate Amalek and to destroy all of their possessions (i.e., the traces of their presence in history). Saul, as we know, did not comply. David massacred them and freed all the prisoners and the booty that the Amalekites had taken earlier (1 Sam. 30). Strangely, the question of booty is again a bone of contention among the Israelites (see vv. 22ff.), and the generosity of David toward the rear guard and the elders of Judah (vv. 26-31) is echoed in Esther (9:19,22). Esther 9 finally repairs Saul's mistake; Haman the Agagite is hanged on the gallows he erected for Mordecai the Jew. That event reorients history.

This is not the end of the road, however, but only a curve. The death of Haman, says Clines, "has solved nothing, relieved nothing. He himself may be dead, but his evil is very much alive. And it lives on under the banner of unalterable Persian law."[68] There are still Hamans in history. After the events of 70 c.e., the Rabbis identified Rome with Amalek, or with his grandfather Esau, thus affirming again the symbolic character of those names. *Pesiqta Rabbati* 47b urges abstaining from hating an Edomite or an

---

67. One can also understand, as does the King James Version, that the Lord *swears* eternal enmity with Amalek. This is, it seems, how *Mekhilta Exod.* read the text of Exod. 17:16. Rabbi Eliezer said, "The Place [God] swore by his throne of glory that, if one of the nations became a proselyte, it will be accepted, but not Amalek and his house." Cf. *Pesiq. R.* 47b. here below.

68. Clines, *Ezra, Nehemiah, Esther,* 18. For Clines, this motif was added later to an original story more or less represented by the A-text in Greek, and which ended with the simple revocation of the edict by the king.

Egyptian; but as to Amalek, "Remember what Amalek did to you." In another Rabbinic text the distinction is based upon the fact that Edomites and Egyptians met Israel with the sword (Num. 20:18), "but with regard to those who sought to make Israel sin [here, Moab and Ammon], it is said that they should never enter the congregation of the Lord (Deut. 23:3)" *(Tanhuma B, Pinehas 76a in fine).* Origen did not miss that archetypal or metaphorical meaning of Amalek. He wrote, "It does not behoove us to spare that invisible Amalek, who withstands those wishing to ascend from Egypt and escape from the darkness of this world into the promised land, and who attacks us" *(Hom. in Num.,* xix, 1; Migne, col. 722, B). He added, "Understand all this to refer to the battles of the saints who wage warfare against sin" *(In Lib. Jesu Nave,* viii, 7; Migne, col. 870, B). Origen's introversion is echoed in the Talmud by a very interesting haggadah in *Sanh.* 99b; Timna wanted to become a proselyte but was rebuked by Abraham, Isaac, and Jacob. Then she became the concubine of Esau's son Eliphaz, for she said, "Better to become a handmaid of this nation than a princess [that she was according to Genesis 36:10, 12, 29] of any other." Her son Amalek "wrought great trouble to Israel. Why? Because they ought not to have repelled her."[69]

But if Haman has historical avatars, so does Mordecai. Esther 10:1-3 focuses upon the enduring good done to his people by Mordecai, "second to king Ahasuerus, great among the Jews, popular with the multitude of his brethren, seeking the good of his people and speaking peace to all his kinsmen" (10:3). This is the last word, a word of peace for all generations. This "again, projects the book beyond the narrated period," so that the story has "inbuilt its own hermeneutical rules, specifying how it is to be read and thus what it really means."[70] This is a real insight. In the perspective that I hold as fundamental for the reading of the book, Esther is invested—in spite of its absence of religiosity— with a considerable theological task.

69. The English translations of most of the Rabbinic texts quoted in this paper are by C. G. Montefiore and H. Loewe, *A Rabbinic Anthology.*
70. Clines, *Ezra, Nehemiah, Esther,* 25.

Therefore it is not inappropriate, I believe, to end this study of the most secular document of the Bible with a liturgical text of the Synagogue. It is a psalm of praise belonging to the celebration of Hanukkah. It says:

> You sustained them in the time of their suffering.
> You embraced their quarrel.
> You made of their right your right,
>   and of their vengeance your vengeance.
> You gave the powerful into the hands of the weak
>   and the numerous to the few,
>   the impure into the hands of the pure,
>   the wicked into the hands of the righteous,
>   and the arrogant into the hands
>   of those who fulfill your Torah.

CHAPTER 6

Ruth

The meaning and significance of some biblical texts, like some works of secular literature, may not depend on their date of composition. A young student of middle-school age may perhaps be excused for not knowing exactly at what epoch *Hamlet* was written, for example. Had the play been composed two centuries earlier or later, little of its meaning and impact would be altered. Not so with the book of Ruth. I shall try to show here that one's view of the purpose of this little literary jewel is entirely different if one holds that it was written after instead of before the Jewish exile in Babylon. In fact, strange as it may sound, even its literary genre depends upon the solution that we give to the chronological question. Johannes Wolfgang von Goethe, who took for granted Ruth's ostensible setting in the time of Judges (see Ruth 1:1), spoke of the book as a delightful idyll.[1] Others, however, who believe that the story is an ad hoc response to the Ezra-Nehemiah reforms, see in the book of Ruth a "novelle," or even a satire (i.e., the opposite of an apologue or an idyll).

Unfortunately, the problem is very complex. Recent studies and commentaries emphasize the classicism and elegance of the language, a fact that leads them to prefer a preexilic date. This, however, is not my stance. On the contrary, the language of the book notwithstanding, I am convinced that Ruth is a brilliant polemical performance under the guise of an antique and innocu-

1. J. W. v. Goethe, *West-östlicher Divan* (1819), in *Göthe's Werke*, 21:231.

ous tale. The discussion of the issue need not be dry or tedious, as it helps us discover a diamond of the rarest quality.

In contrast to Susanna, Judith, and Esther, there are no villains in Ruth, and this feature has repeatedly been taken by critics as "proving" the irenic, nonpolemical character of the story. A postexilic parallel is, however, provided by the book of Jonah, where the would-be villains repent as one man. That book is a subtle onslaught against the isolationists in power at Jerusalem, but the "adversaries" are snubbed by indirection only, and in something of a respectful mood.[2] There is in Ruth the same absence of harshness vis-à-vis coreligionists whose interpretation of election is wrong. In their opinion, God has given up all hope of repentance of the nations. This brings them to leave the non-Jew in outer darkness. In the same way that the object of the book of Jonah is to denounce their lack of "prophetic" spirit of generosity, the object of the book of Ruth is to describe the model of faithfulness displayed by a Moabitess, and how providential it is that she was accepted and even honored by her contemporary Israelites. She became the great-grandmother of King David.

It is for this reason and no other that the author belabors the point of Ruth's foreignness (Ruth 1:4,22; 2:2,6,10-13,21; 4:5, 10). As stated by Dorothea Harvey, "The adjective 'Moabitess' appears at least twice in connection with Ruth where the plot does not demand the title (2:2,21)."[3] This issue is crucial to the purpose of the tale. Ruth is not any foreigner in general. She belongs to a nation that, for Israel, represents perversion and destruction. Numbers 22ff. (see especially 25:1ff.) explains the origin of the hostility between the two peoples. Moabite females attempted to corrupt the Israelites coming from Egypt on their way to Canaan. Since then, the numerous references to Moab in Scriptures are unanimously pejorative. Zephaniah 2:9 (seventh century B.C.E.) exclaims, "Surely Moab shall be as Sodom!" Deuteronomy 23:2-6) prohibits Ammonites and Moabites from ever

---

2. See A. and P. E. LaCocque, *The Jonah Complex,* and *Jonah, the Prophet and the Complex.*
3. D. Harvey, "Book of Ruth," 133.

entering the community of Israel. Even the Edomites are treated more kindly (Deut. 23:7-8).[4]

It is of particular interest to see that very ostracism of the Moabites reaffirmed in unequivocal terms by the fifth-century Ezra and Nehemiah. Ezra 9:1 speaks of the abominations of the Moabites. Nehemiah 13:1 reminds the returnees "that an Ammonite and a Moabite shall not enter into the assembly of God for ever." In the same chapter, Nehemiah reviles those among the Israelites who married Moabite women.

Already on that score, it would be very strange that in all those invectives against Moab, no provision is made for the Moabite ancestry of King David, had it been an established archaic tradition. Nothing of the sort happens. On the contrary, down to the time of the Midrash, the situation described by the book of Ruth is received with great embarrassment by the Rabbis. They struggle hard to reconcile the irreconcilable in the texts, and the Talmud finally decides that the Deuteronomic condemnation of Moab applies to males only.[5] That is, Ezra 9:1-2 and Neh. 13:1, 23ff. are conveniently bypassed.

Were it just a legal issue, the Talmud has every right to interpret the old law with a lenient spirit. But the book of Ruth goes much further than establishing a point of jurisprudence. Not only is a Moabitess entering the assembly of Israel, but the law of levirate marriage is applied to her—a law that, most evidently, was meant to protect the Israelite family from extinction and Israelite property from dispersion. I shall return to this custom below, but it is important already here to stress its strictly internal nature in Israel. Few other legal customs in Scriptures could compete with the levirate in its Israelite specificity and typicality. We can easily imagine that, in the eyes of purists, the application of the levirate to a Moabite widow would constitute an aberration.

As if it were not scandalous enough, the story uses the term

<hr />

4. M. Eliade keenly remarks, "The struggle against the false gods begins immediately after the escape from the desert, at Baal-Peor. It is there that the daughters of the Moabitess invite the Israelites to the sacrifices to their gods . . . (Num. 25:2ff.). . . . For Israel this struggle, begun at Baal-Peor, still continues." *A History of Religious Ideas,* 1:180–81.

5. See *m. Yad.* 4:4; 8:3; *Tos. Yad.* 2.17. See above chapter 4, "Judith," n. 13.

ḥesed (steadfast love) in speaking of Ruth in 3:10. The word appears in 1:8 and 2:20 to describe God's fidelity and trustworthiness. Moreover, elsewhere in Scripture, *ḥesed* designates the contractual attitude of loyalty and love within the framework of covenant. It is striking in that context that Naomi starts by expressing bitterness in view of the failure of the covenant as far as she is concerned. It appears that the line of Elimelech must end. Her complaint, however, slowly turns to hope as events unwind, with Ruth in the center (see 2:20). By the third chapter, Naomi can advise Ruth to adopt an open-minded attitude, so to speak, and to let things work out almost by themselves. Eventually, it becomes clear that YHWH has remained faithful to Naomi, and a chorus of village women declare in the final chapter, "A son is born to Naomi!"

But the *ḥesed* of God to Naomi materializes in the *ḥesed* of Ruth the Moabitess. In Nelson Glueck's definition, *ḥesed* is something beyond an attitude of obligation. This, as we shall see below, is crucial for the understanding of Ruth's role in the tale. But, it is again and more than ever an aberration in the eyes of orthodoxy so untypically to broaden the scope of *ḥesed* to cover a semantic field so vast that it risks relativizing the formally precise meaning of the word. Far from having a universalistic sense, the term describes the intimate relationship between God and his people (Hos. 4:1). Is now a Moabitess a model of fidelity for Israel? That is exactly what the author of Ruth is saying.[6]

In 2:12, Boaz's admiration for Ruth is based on her unselfish efforts to perpetuate an Israelite name even though she is a Moabitess. On the model of other similar "recapitulations" of aborted events of the past that we came across above, particularly about Esther, Ruth in this text redeems the tragic failure of the first encounter between Israel and her people on the "plains of Moab" (Num. 22:1).[7]

---

6. "God's love, like all true love, operates in a world not of cause and effect but of freedom and gratuitousness. . . . The world outside the fence is the world of gratuitousness, it is there that God dwells . . ." (G. Gutierrez, *On Job,* 87).

7. See below apropos Ruth 2:12 and Ruth 3. Postexilic midrashic reuse of

Oswald Loretz has proposed that the object of the book of Ruth is the threat of extinction of an Israelite family, therefore of its "name." The threat is changed through peripety (turn of fortune) into preservation of the name. This latter is even granted the most brilliant future, as the line thus perpetuated leads to the birth of King David.[8] Peripety, of course, as in Esther, goes hand in hand with happy coincidence. That is what the word *miqreh* stresses in Ruth 2:3. It can be translated, with the New English Bible, "as it happened," or, as the word is used here with a possessive pronoun and accompanies a verb of the same root, "her fate made her happen [upon a parcel of land belonging to Boaz]."[9] Along the same line, the book's use of *we-hinneh,* "and just then," in 2:4; 3:8, and 4:1 provides an element of surprise or chance.

The issue of name preservation cannot be fully developed until the levirate marriage is examined (see below). But Loretz's suggestion receives a partial confirmation in the motif of Naomi's lament. This narrative element that puts in motion the whole story "is second to none among the laments of the Old Testament women who have been deprived of motherhood."[10] Such elegiac accents recall those of Rachel in Gen. 30:1 or of Hannah in 1 Sam. 1:5.[11] It will be seen later how such parallels with the matriarchs in Israel play an important role in the book of Ruth.

If indeed the object of the story is a question of name perpetuation—a statement that is only partially true, as we shall see—the problem of authenticity, hence of literary genre, becomes a pres-

---

ancient texts frees them from their provisionary impasse and brings them to their fulfillment. In Jonah, Nineveh is the Sodom of Genesis 19 (cf. Jon. 1:1-2 and Gen. 18:21-22; in Jonah 3 the verb *haphakh,* "overthrow," is technical, in reference to the overthrowing of Sodom and Gomorrah: Gen. 19:21,25,29, and other biblical texts; Jon. 3:5 and Gen. 19:4,11, "from the young to the old," and "from the least to the greatest"). Conversely, while at the rising of the sun Sodom is a smoking ruin (Gen. 19:15,24-29), Jonah is dismayed that this did not happen for Nineveh (Jon. 4:7-8). It is perhaps this reversal of situation that brought the reversal of expressions in Jonah, where are found "from great to small" and "herd and flock." A parallel is provided by the movement of repentance in Jonah 3, which goes from the masses up to the king.

8. O. Loretz, "The Theme of the Ruth Story."
9. Rabbi Meir Zlotowitz, *Megillas Ruth* (1976), ad loc.
10. Loretz, "The Theme of the Ruth Story," 393.
11. Hannah is very much on the mind of the author of Ruth, as 4:15 proves (Ruth "is better to you than seven sons"). Cf. 1 Sam. 1:9.

sing one. Is Ruth pure fiction or is it based on historical facts? In particular, it is clear that the depiction in Ruth of a Mobite ancestry for David is highly problematic. Wilhelm Rudolph, however, probably goes too far when he writes, "It is out of the question that a tale would have invented a Moabite grandmother for the greatest and most celebrated king of Israel, prototype of the Messiah. Therefore, this central narrative affirmation must be historical."[12]

Another unwarranted conclusion about David's ancestry is drawn by other critics, among them E. F. Campbell and R. M. Hals.[13] A Moabite great-grandmother for David would be unthinkable at the time of the Deuteronomistic historian. His veneration for David went side by side with his hatred of the Moabite (see Deut. 23:3). Hence, say those critics, Ruth must predate the Deuteronomist.

To Rudolph, one can retort that the point is not whether or not David historically had a Moabite grandmother. The book of Ruth does not make an objective historical point. It says that without the Moabitess there would have been no "greatest and most celebrated king of Israel, prototype of the Messiah." That is, without the Moabitess, history would be like a wadi whose waters have dried up. Ruth, furthermore, was not just a passive instrument for the preservation of the ancestral line of David; she was a beacon of *ḥesed* (faith, loyalty) for Israel, a woman to rank with the matriarchs of the nation.[14]

That such a story need not be pre-Deuteronomic but is a reaction to a conservative party inspired by the Deuteronomic and the Priestly works as appropriated by Ezra-Nehemiah and successors is, I believe, no far-fetched possibility. It is the stance that I defend here. We are thus sent back to square one, so to speak, and the problems of genre and date are as acute as ever.

Already in 1913, Hermann Gunkel stressed the difference be-

12. W. Rudolph, *Das Buch Ruth,* 7. That Rudolph is most probably wrong is indicated by the genealogy of Matthew 1. The latter shows that (probably late) tradition included at least one other surprising element to David's ancestry. The Canaanite harlot Rahab figures among David's grandmothers! Here again, it would be futile to look for a historical confirmation of that assertion.

13. E. F. Campbell, Jr., *Ruth;* R. M. Hals, *Theology of the Book of Ruth.*

14. In the Jewish Haggadah, Ruth is counted among "the mothers of Israel" (*Ruth R.* 1:14; *P.K.* 16, 124a).

tween historical report focusing upon events, and story depicting "the situations and the delineation of the characters" *(Seelenleben).*[15] Gunkel astutely perceived the highly important shift from reporting of fact to character exposition, particularly through direct speech. This, said the German critic, is a new genre best termed "novelle." The characters themselves indirectly voice the author's feelings, "somewhat like the chorus in Greek tragedy." Robert Alter also emphasizes this "minimal authorial intervention," which he sees as "the theologically appropriate means for the representatives of human lives under the overarching dominion of an ultimately unknowable but ethical God."[16]

This point is all-important. As the story excludes the self-reference of the narrator, so that "the events themselves seem to tell their own story,"[17] we are left unable to determine whether the narrated past is reality or fiction. The problem is the harder to solve since, on the one hand, Ruth presents itself as a historical, nonfictional narrative, but, on the other hand, the reference marks are only marginal to the plot. Truth in a literary narrative is characterized by specific authorial indications—for example, the discussion of historical documents. In the book of Ruth, however, the alleged traces of history's steps lack specificity. They are geographical (Moab, Bethlehem), cultural (levirate marriage), onomastic (Naomi, Boaz), genealogical (ancestry of David). The latter could be decisive, but, on the contrary, it raises our suspicion. After all, despite Rudolph's certainty as to its historicity, it could be a fictional speculation based on 1 Sam. 22:3-4, which shows there were ties between David and Moab.

It is thus probably better to adopt Campbell's characterization of the tale as "a Hebrew short story," that is, without historical claim. As this genre developed in the early monarchic period, or even earlier, during the time of the Judges, when "the patriarchal narratives took their form," Ruth's purpose, according to Campbell, would be to tell the people "of their king's humble origins."[18]

15. H. Gunkel, *Reden und Aufsätze,* 65, 84.
16. R. Alter, *Art of Biblical Narrative,* 86–87.
17. Emile Benveniste, *Problèmes de linguistique générale,* 241. ("Les événements semblent se raconter d'eux-mêmes.")
18. Campbell, "The Hebrew Short Story: A Study of Ruth," 92.

But this is very improbable. In a popular tale contemporary with the glorious reign of David, we would expect a grandiose description at the very confines of myth and legend. The people were not looking for anything that cast a shadow on the nobility of their king. Rather, their sense of belonging with David to a grand destiny would express itself in a legend flattering their sense of identity and nationalism. True, one could evoke a story like that of Cinderella, which obviously is no invitation to humility on the model of "the girl in ashes," but a human projection of the desire to "make it big," like the blameless heroine's accession from rags to riches. In that case, Ruth would drive home the same message. But the success of tales like Cinderella lies in the stark contrast they build between the original dereliction of the hero or heroine and his or her final triumph. Ruth, however, has no business drawing such a contrast. The heroine is from the start a noble character, saluted by Boaz as displaying an unusual *hesed* although she comes from Moab. Because of that, she is welcomed in her new community—with various degrees of enthusiasm, it is true, and this precisely is decisive. The story is no mirror of Judaean pride during the Davidic empire, but of the deep split between Palestinian parties during the Second Commonwealth.

At stake in the discussion of date are diametrically opposed interpretations of Ruth. Either the tale is a preexilic apologue or it is a postexilic parable. Apologue sets an ethical model; its purpose is edification and confirmation of world.[19] Parable questions ideology; it subverts world.

I have mentioned above the classicism of Ruth's language. In and of itself it could be an indication of antiquity. But the question is far from settled. There are, in the first place, peculiarities of vocabulary and syntax, an indication that the book might belong after all to late Hebrew literature, of which one characteristic is linguistic imitation of older works. Be that as it may, it is probable that the linguistic argument must be abandoned for now as proof one way or the other.[20] There remains as a second

---

19. For G. Fohrer, *Introduction to the Old Testament*, 251, the purpose of Ruth is "edification."

20. The presence in a given text of antique words, syntactic forms, and stylistic turns does not prove the text's antiquity. However, the presence in a text of *new* words, syntactic simplifications, and stylistic novelties certainly does make it a late production.

clue the demonstrated poetic skill of the author of Ruth, who can put into the mouths of older characters of the tale archaizing solemn verbal forms that no younger personages in the story use.[21] Third, also on the plane of stylistic features typical of postexilic period, Ruth's style is anthological. There is, for example, an exact correspondence between the rhetoric in Ruth 1:1 and Gen. 12:10; Ruth 2:20 and Gen. 24:27.[22] Fourth, if indeed Ruth is a postexilic work, we are less surprised to discover in the book the presence of a phenomenon common to the narratives of that late period: their "theology" is strikingly devoid of religious jargon. About Ruth, E. Campbell rightly remarks, "God's activity in the Ruth book is very much that of the one in the shadows."[23] Of the Joseph *novella,* a late composition in the book of Genesis,[24] it has been noted by André Neher that God's speaking is absent from 37:1 to 46:2.[25] In Job, the situation is more complex. The proper name of God is replaced by substitutes such as El, Eloah, Elohim, El Shaddai—until YHWH speaks at the end and brings a denouement to the aporia of justice on earth. The prime example is provided by the book of Esther—and now Ruth. All those stories—to which could be added others such as Jonah, where the prophetic oracle, five words in Hebrew, is singularly areligious—occur in a foreign place or with foreigners. Job is an Edomite in Edom. He eventually becomes an intercessor for other Edomites, his "friends" (see 42:8). Joseph goes into Egypt and becomes a savior for both his kin and the Egyptians. Esther is queen of Persia and accomplishes a work of salvation on behalf of her people and the Persians. Jonah goes to Assyria and, albeit reluctantly, saves Nineveh. Ruth is also savior in a "foreign" land that happens to be none else than Israel! We shall develop this point later in this chapter.

With respect to the setting, the understated language on reli-

21. P. Humbert, *Opuscules d'un hébraïsant,* 92 n.
22. J. L. Vesco, "La date du livre de Ruth." Cf. J. Gray, *Joshua, Judges and Ruth,* 400.
23. Campbell, *Ruth,* 28.
24. See, for example, D. B. Redford, *A Study of the Biblical Story of Joseph, Genesis 37–50;* J. van Seters, *Abraham in History and Tradition,* 68.
25. Neher, *Exile of the Word,* 29. See "Esther" above, 61.

gious matters, the synergism of human agents with God and often the latter's conspicuous absence, the role of underdogs and women in bringing about (partial) fulfillments of *Heilsgeschichte*—all point to a common stock of *subversive* authors. A work of salvation done on behalf of Israel by a Moabitess is as scandalous as a work of salvation performed by an Israelite prophet on behalf of Nineveh! Ruth is no apologue.

We cannot take leave of the question of genre without mixing our voice with those who praise the extraordinary literary achievement of the book of Ruth. The style is flawless, displaying a refinement rarely paralleled before or after. "Every phrase [is] as though it sprouted by itself, without the slightest difficulty of expression—all natural and yet bearing the stamp of artistic perfection."[26]

One of the most successful attempts at grasping the superb melodious accents of the story is the comparison, by Bezalel Porten and Evelyn Strouse, with a musical sonata:

> The resemblance to a classical sonata is exact. The first half is an exposition of the subject of death (in various forms: of the land, of husband and sons, of a family name), with a transitional passage toward the other theme, restoration; the second half develops the idea of restoration, recapitulates both themes, and adds a coda.[27]

There is a resolution of the narrative tension through the levirate marriage of the Moabitess with the *go'el* of Elimelech's family, Boaz. Such a denouement was the most appropriate because the author wanted to bring the story as close as possible to the episode of Judah and Tamar in Genesis 38. There, the Canaanite Tamar shrinks from nothing to obtain justice according to legal custom, as her father-in-law, Judah, seems to have resolved not to provide her with one of his sons to give a posthumous issue to her deceased husband.[28]

There are three texts in Scripture that illustrate the levirate

26. Jacob Fichman, *'Arugot* (1954), 282–86, quoted and translated in *The Hebrew Bible in Literary Criticism,* 540.

27. B. Porten and E. Strouse, "A Reading of Ruth," 63, quoted and translated in *The Hebrew Bible in Literary Criticism,* 545.

28. One will notice the perfect parallel between the Canaanite Tamar and the Moabitess Ruth, both determined to perpetuate an Israelite family and/or name.

marriage: Genesis 38, Deut. 25:5-10, and Ruth 4. There are grave discrepancies between the legal picture given by the narrative of Ruth and that of Deuteronomy in particular. As far as the Deuteronomic law is concerned, the conditions of the marriage are severely limited. It takes place when the widow is childless and the deceased has a marriageable brother living in the same house. The marriage is for the sole purpose of begetting a son, who legally will be the deceased's son and thus inherit his legal father's property. It seems that the connubium ceases immediately when the woman is pregnant. The law does not stipulate this, but Judah is said not to have continued going in to Tamar. In addition, the levirate marriage is presented as a legal duty, not as a right, to perpetuate a "name" in Israel. There is nothing romantic or charitable in the custom.

In Ruth, there is no question of a brother living in the same house. Ruth's husband's brother also died in Moab. Another jarring peculiarity is that in the law the living brother is called a *yabam, levir,* a word that in Hebrew seems to have meant "progenitor."[29] In Ruth, however, the next of kin (or his substitute Boaz) is not called *yabam,* but *go'el.*[30] The action of *ge'ulah,* Robert Gordis pointedly states, is "the restoration of an object to its primal condition."[31] *Go'el* is often translated "redeemer," but sometimes the context demands the rendition "avenger" or "counselor." At any rate, in Ruth the accent has certainly shifted to a different set of the levir's duties. The levirate marriage is now more of a right of the widow and meant for her comfort or welfare. That switching movement had been inaugurated by Genesis 38, the story in that text being entirely based upon Tamar's right to remarry a son of Judah. More than a "progenitor" in the sense of Deuteronomy 25, Ruth after Tamar needs a "restorer" *(go'el).*[32] Tamar must be vindicated in her femininity

---

29. At Ugarit, Anat is called *ybmt l'mm* (procreator), and in Arabic *wabama* is "to procreate." See K-B, s.v. *ybm.*

30. *Ruth,* however, uses the term *yebamah,* as does Deut. 25:7,9, to designate the brother's widow, or the widow of the brother of a wife's husband; Ruth 1:15 (two times). This term, situated at the start of the story, is like a signpost indicating the central importance of the custom of levirate marriage for the plot. See below.

31. R. Gordis, "Love, Marriage, and Business in the Book of Ruth," 253.

32. See discussion of Lev. 25:25, below.

and in her membership by exogamy to the clan of Judah. The correspondent in Ruth to Shelah, who was not granted to Tamar, is "So and so," that anonymous man who forfeits his "rights" and thereby frustrates Ruth/Naomi's "rights."

Thus, by artistic transpositions, Tamar the Canaanite becomes Ruth the Moabite, and Judah's sons or Judah himself become "So and so." The symbolism is transparent; the postexilic Judahites of the exclusivist party in Jerusalem are put on a par with Shelah or with Onan. They sterilize history and put it in desperate need of a "strong man," of a "Bo-az" (in him is power) to revitalize it. The author of Ruth drew that stark parallel with Genesis 38 for many reasons, some of which are already clear at this point; others will be discussed below. No definition of the levirate marriage, however innovative, could entirely accommodate the needs of the poet. It was particularly difficult to advocate such a set of duties and rights when a Moabitess was at the center of the affair. Furthermore, when Boaz married Ruth it was not for the sole purpose of begetting one child, after which, so to speak, the marriage would dissolve. Boaz and Ruth are to remain husband and wife.

The book of Ruth complicates the problem of levirate marriage in bringing to the fore not one but two interrelated widowed women, Naomi and Ruth. The levirate is supposed to work for both in this case, and even more so for Naomi than for Ruth, because the latter is of Moab and therefore is not protected by Israelite endogamic laws. Moreover, the son of Ruth, Obed, represents not so much the continuation of the name of Ruth's husband, Mahlon, as the continuation of Naomi's. Therefore, the levirate as understood by Ruth is even more far-fetched than is usually recognized by scholars, for Naomi is not a widow without child but a widow who lost her children before they could beget successors. As she cannot bear other children at her age (Ruth 1:11), the *ge'ulah* is inapplicable to her (1:12-13), and the impasse seems total.

It is at this point that an unforeseen element reverses the situation. Ruth, Naomi's daughter-in-law, shuns the possibility of staying in her country and remarrying there with a Moabite of her age in order to start another line, a Moabite line. She decides to cling to her mother-in-law *and to the Israelite line* that her deceased husband had been unable to perpetuate. In the most moving declaration of loyalty in the Bible, she tells Naomi: "Wherever you go, I shall go; where you stay, I shall stay. Your people are my people, and your God is my God" (1:16). Although Ruth undoubtedly has a profound affection for her mother-in-law, her declaration goes deeper than the level of feelings. There is here an appropriation by Ruth of Naomi's existence and fate, and a disappropriation of her own. "All that is mine is yours, and all that is yours remains yours."[33] This offering of herself becomes in the story a veritable substitution.[34]

Levirate marriage is inapplicable to Naomi, but Ruth will act in such a way that it will apply. It involves a property that will serve as a transition to the real issue. The field of Naomi, which we readers are surprised to learn about so late in the story (Ruth 4:3), raises a problem. First, the field is "Elimelech's" (4:3) and, with one exception, no legal texts in the Bible indicate that widows inherit from their deceased husbands. The contrary is suggested by Num. 27:9-11. Campbell has seen the difficulty and adduces 2 Kings 8:1-6 as a parallel.[35] But the Shunammite widow had a living son! It is to her, not to Naomi, that Neufeld's category of "executrix or trustee" (for her male heir) applies.[36] In the absence of a son, however, Naomi has nobody for whom she could function as trustee in managing her husband's field. Rather, therefore, we should see in Ruth's matter-of-fact statement that Naomi inherited Elimelech's field a sign of later times, when indeed women experienced some kind of emancipation.[37] In any case, the purchase of Naomi's field by a next of kin

33. This is Martin Buber's characterization of Hasidic love.

34. Interestingly enough, the notion is not absent in the Ruth text. Ruth 4:7 deals with customs regarding *ge'ulah* and *temurah,* used synonymously in Leviticus 27. The word *temurah* appears only in those texts and in Job 15:31; 20:18; 28:17. It means "(things acquired by) exchange" (see K-B).

35. Campbell, *Ruth,* 157–58.

36. E. Neufeld, *Ancient Hebrew Marriage Laws* (London and New York: Longmans, Green, and Co., 1944) 240f. Quoted by H. H. Rowley, *The Servant of the Lord and Other Essays on the Old Testament,* 175.

37. In the Jewish colony of Elephantine in the fifth century B.C.E. widows inherited from their husbands, but it took a long time for this right to come ashore in Palestine, and it did not remain unchallenged. It is probable that only progressive milieus in Judah of the Second Commonwealth agreed with woman's emancipation.

remains highly improbable, since it implies for the buyer the disbursement of money for something that would eventually become his anyway at the death of the widow, in the absence of a direct heir. Only in the case of "a son born to *Naomi"* (4:17) would the field legally return to support her, until her son would be able to inherit and exploit it. The transaction at the gate is provoked by Boaz's challenging the nonintervention by those who could redeem the field and thus help the widow with the purchase money. If "So and so" does not buy the field, he, Boaz, will do it and deprive the one "first in line" of his greed's easy prey. Boaz forces the issue; he coerces "So and so" to make a move, either in buying the field he thought he would get free of charge, or in eschewing his rights. The first move of "So and so" is to purchase from Naomi the piece of property that belongs to the clan of Elimelech, of which he himself is a member. It is in a way a generous move, but also and above all it is a dutiful act according to the law. In Lev. 25:25-28 we find the stipulation regarding the redemption of property: "If your brother becomes poor, and sells part of his property, then his next of kin shall come and redeem *(ga'al)* what his brother has sold" (v. 25). D. R. G. Beattie is probably right in suggesting that redeeming the property of a kinsman did not mean that the redeemer held absolute title to the property.[38]

At any rate, "So and so's" first move is to fulfill the law as far as the property is concerned. But then, Boaz tells him, he becomes the *go'el* and consequently the *levir.* He must take the female owner with her field; not Naomi, to be sure, but Ruth, who by substitution represents Naomi and fills the conditions for carrying a direct heir to Naomi's name. "So and so" is unwilling to fulfill this double duty, if only because of the financial burden that this represents: the repurchase of a property and the support of a woman who, being a foreigner, has nothing of her own to bring in as a wedding present. That, he says, "would spoil my inheritance," as the land would revert in due time to Ruth's child or, more accurately, to Naomi's child whom she might legally

---

38. D. R. G. Beattie, "The Book of Ruth as Evidence for Israel's Legal practice."

"adopt" as her own, as indeed the story shows that she does with Obed (see Ruth 4:16).

Thus, the situation rhetorically envisaged in Ruth 1:12 ceases in due time to be rhetorical and becomes actual. "So and so" is facing a totally unexpected development. Buying the field of Naomi made sense, for Naomi was too old to have children and therefore must not be taken as wife in fulfillment of the levirate law (even very broadly interpreted). But now, Naomi is replaced by a young woman, so that serving as *go'el* of Naomi's property—not too bad a business—means also serving as *levir* to Ruth—potentially a disastrous affair.

That "So and so" thinks twice before committing himself to such a deal is all the more understandable since, with Ruth the foreigner, an entirely new situation obtains in relation to the classic levirate marriage. We have seen above that the purpose is to provide one male heir to the deceased. It is not a definitive marriage, and, logically, the *levir* is not to continue to have intercourse with the woman. In the Sanskrit Laws of Manu, section 62 reads, "But when the purpose of the appointment to cohabit with the widow has been attained in accordance with the law, these two shall behave towards each other like a father and daughter-in-law."[39]

It is clear that the levirate was seen as bordering on incest, and it is for good reason that Judah refrains from going in to Tamar after the conception of a child. But, in the case of "So and so" marrying Ruth, there would be no danger of incest and the levirate marriage would become an actual and permanent marriage. Furthermore, the son born from that union would be both son of Elimelech legally (i.e., son of Naomi, his widow) *and* son of the actual father. The story shows that Obed is both "son of Naomi" *and* "son of Boaz." It is again attested by the genealogy that serves as a coda to the story. Hence "So and so" is right in thinking that the arrangement would jeopardize the inheritance that he wants to leave behind after his death.

---

39. Quoted by Thomas and Dorothy Thompson, "Some Legal Problems in the Book of Ruth," 95. The area where the levirate marriage was practiced is expansive. Beside the Sanskrit, it is also documented in Assyrian, Hittite, Hurrite, Elamite, and Ugaritic laws.

We encounter another surprise: Obed is called Naomi's *go'el* (4:17). Ruth's bodily substitution for Naomi as a wife is paralleled by Naomi's substitution for Ruth as a mother. And now, Boaz's *ge'ulah* shifts to his son Obed. This last transposition has a clear motivation. Boaz has become the *go'el* and *levir* of Ruth representing Naomi. But he really is such for Naomi in the person of his son. Obed is Naomi's *go'el* because his birth cancels out all prerequisite conditions to her ownership of the family's property. T. and D. Thompson appropriately say, to preserve a "name" in Israel means property as well as name. The keeping of the name is "the effort to keep progeny and property (name and person) together"[40] (see 2 Sam. 14:7). Before Obed is born, however, Boaz serves as *go'el,* and he buys Naomi's land "until someone is able to redeem that land and return it to the family of Elimelech."[41] That someone is Obed.

A whole theological perspective opens up before us on the theme of substitution. For the self-giving of Ruth emphasizes a certain approach to historical course that we need to explore further. We may, for instance, contrast the attitude of Ruth with that of Judith, who penetrates like a sword into the heart of the enemy camp and beheads its captain. Judith is a political paradigm; Ruth is quite another one. In both cases, the odds against them are formidable. In both, also, the outcome retrospectively justifies the initial option. Vulnerability, however, distances the response of Ruth from the genre of epic, so popular because of the natural desire of the crowd to identify with heroes. On the literary score as well, the odds are against the story of Ruth, and misunderstandings are possible. That the narrative of Ruth is so attractive to its readers is a tribute to the mastery of the poet. He or she succeeded in making Ruth and her self-effacement stir the imagination.

There is heroism here, however, of another kind. Without Ruth, Naomi would be a widow without support, without property (at least for all practical purposes), without goal in life ("call me Marah, Bitter," she says on her way back to Bethlehem). The

40. Ibid., 87.
41. Ibid., 99.

Jewess without the Moabitess is but deadwood. Written in the time of Ezra and Nehemiah, the story is a politically subversive pamphlet. No one with the desire to shock his or her Israelite readership could have chosen a "hero" more controversial, even repulsive, than a woman from Moab. Moreover, as if it were not scandalous enough to have that personage of the drama helping and, literally, nourishing an Israelite, the story intends to show that the sociopolitical tension introduced by the unwelcome presence of the foreigner in the community will be resolved, not by the expulsion but by the marriage of the Moabitess with Boaz, the *go'el* (redeemer) of Elimelech's family, thus granting to Ruth the vindication of her initial choice (chap. 1).

It is out of the question that Ruth is described in the story as looking for the satisfaction of her sexual drives or of her right to be a mother. It is, to the contrary, her self-forgetfulness that Boaz admires so much in the threshing-floor scene. There, as we shall see below, she puts herself in a most compromising situation— but not for selfish purposes. The issue is the perpetuation of an Israelite name. On that score, Ruth is perfectly consistent with the Deuteronomic law. Deuteronomy 25:5-10 three times mentions "Israel."

Even within the context of the Israelite community, when all ideal conditions are considered, it must be acknowledged that the legal stipulations to the *levir* demand from him a genuine generosity and self-sacrifice. For he is to provide someone else an heir to ancestral property. From that perspective, it is understandable that the levirate is "the only law in the Pentateuch in which public disgrace is enjoined as a penalty."[42] The disgrace is signified by a gesture of contempt on the part of the widow, who removes the failing brother's sandal and spits in his face. The removal of the sandal is so ignominious that it extends to the man's house as a whole, which is from then on called "The House of the Unsandalled Man" (Deut. 25:10).

An example of (disguised) refusal is provided by Onan precisely in the story of Tamar. T. and D. Thompson have astutely

---

42. C. M. Carmichael, "A Ceremonial Crux: Removing a Man's Sandal as a Female Gesture of Contempt."

shown that Onan prevents Tamar from being free because he ostensibly does what is necessary to give an offspring to his deceased brother while in fact trying to steal his inheritance. When Judah later sends Tamar to live with her father, Judah still keeps authority over her, for he can condemn her to being burned alive for adultery while having no intention of providing a *levir* to her from among his sons. Tamar is thus doubly flouted.

In the story of Ruth, the legal opprobrium is somewhat softened as far as "So and so" is concerned. There are even those who say that the removal of his sandal has very little to do anymore with the ignominy envisaged by Deuteronomy.[43] It remains true that the explicit and implicit laws and customs in the book of Ruth reveal a complex pattern of societal relationships. It is hard to believe that such a complex legal maze was imagined by the author of Ruth for poetic needs only. It is likely that the narrator alludes to a situation of long ago in Israel when all those intricate substitutions and correspondences were possible. Genesis 38 was still built against such a backdrop. In comparison, Deuteronomy 25, by piling up conditions for its fulfillment, is a far cry from the ancestral custom and is clearly a giant step toward the phasing out of the levirate. Finally, P does not mention it, either in the Holiness Code or in the Priestly Code. Leviticus 18:16 and 20:21 declare that any intercourse between a man and his brother's wife is incest. Numbers 27:1-11 and 36:2-12 tell us that daughters can inherit from their fathers. Those texts, says Adolphe Lods, date from ca. 445 B.C.E. and show that the party of Ezra was opposed to the levirate.[44] This point is crucial to the understanding of Ruth's purpose.

The image of the levirate in our story reflects exactly the distance between the alleged and the real chronology of the book of Ruth. For the sake of the thematic plot, the author had to tell the story against the ostensible background of olden times, when the levirate was not restricted to the improbable presence in the deceased husband's house of a brother living there, marriageable, morally and physically open to (temporary) polygamy, and finan-

---

43. On the mistaken opinion of some who see in the removal of the sandal in Ruth a contract ratification, see below.
44. A. Lods, *Histoire de la littérature hébraïque et juive,* 573ff.

cially well-to-do enough to not be ruined by such a potentially disastrous business. The author of Ruth "revitalized" the ancient custom then obsolete, because he or she wanted to set up a highly paradoxical occurrence. If, at the time of the composition of Ruth, a text such as Deuteronomy 25 was the expression of the law, then it here undergoes a thorough reinterpretation. "Brethren dwelling together" (v. 5) must be understood very broadly as designating kinsmen living in the same land. "Having no child" implies that the living brother is ready not to let his own progeny interfere with his duty as *levir*. The latter term, in Hebrew *yabam* (Deut. 25:5, 7; cf. Gen. 38:3) must see its meaning extended to being a synonym of *go'el* (restorer of welfare, peace, name, status, property). Hence the expression (in Ruth 4:7), "Now this was [the custom] in former times in Israel," does not betray an antiquarian interest of the author, but is a way to stress the authority of a venerable law disregarded by the exclusivist party in Jerusalem.

Ruth's argumentation is that all parts make a whole: the levirate laws, the customs about redeeming and substituting, the matters of inheritance, the gleaning rights of the poor, the right of the non-Jew to become a member of the Israelite community, the duty to restore a widow in her *shalom,* and the restoration of the Davidic line. A noble Israelite marries a Moabitess *in obedience to the law of Moses,* thus invalidating the legal ostracism against Moabites (Deut. 23:3-6), exactly as Judith would do in the second century B.C.E. regarding Ammonites, as we saw in chapter 3. Boaz's obedience and fulfillment of Torah was blessed by heaven, for the outcome was none else than King David himself, so much admired and praised by the ideologists in Jerusalem.[45]

---

45. As can be seen, I do not agree with Mieke Bal's interpretation here (see: *Lethal Love: Feminist Literary Readings of Biblical Love Stories,* 80f.). True, there is tension "between law and legitimacy" (81), but the texts of Deuteronomy 22:22 and 23:2 (Hebrew, 23:3) do not apply to the scene of the trial at the gate; at most, they would apply to the ambiguous scene on the threshing floor. At the gate, both law *and* legitimacy are guaranteed by the elders, whose role it is to establish legitimacy through obedience to the law, not through its transgression (Bal, 81–82). Clearly, the problem at the gate is not whether a man may under certain circumstances "lie with a married woman" and get away with it, but whether the law of levirate applies to Naomi and/or Ruth, and in what way. Deuteronomy 22:22 and 23:3 envisage a case of fornication

The author of Ruth was too refined a person to indulge in invectives against the hierocrats. Rather than giving a name to the first of kin who forfeits his duties as *go'el,* in a story where the names are highly symbolical, the author left him nameless. He is "So and so," an absence of status that begs for identification but at least avoids derogation. (The Midrash cannot resist the temptation to fill the yawning gap; his name was Tov.)[46] Similarly, Ruth herself does not remove his sandal and does not spit in his face, as Deuteronomy 25 said. It was inconceivable that a Moabitess would debase and curse an Israelite while affirming at the same time, "Your people shall be my people" (1:16). At any rate, the removal of the shoe here is not, as it has been said, merely a signature under a contract of sale of property. "So and so" does not buy or sell anything. Boaz, who buys Naomi's field and marries Ruth, does not remove his sandal to seal the contract. Here also, in Deuteronomy 25, the gesture is to be seen within the context of *ge'ulah.*

In fact, the shoe is rich in symbolism. It is to be added to the relatively short list of sexual metaphors that are found in the Bible, alongside of "eating," "shame," "knee," "legs," "feet" . . . . Ludwig Levy has shown the quasi-universal erotic meaning of the foot as a masculine symbol, and of the sandal as a feminine symbol.[47] A woman removing a man's shoe meant that she was breaking the (potential or actual) marriage relationship and claiming to be free to marry another man. Not surprisingly, the symbol is polyvalent. To get hold of the sandal may have the double meaning of having a wife *and* property or authority. It

(crystal-clear in the following verses, which Bal [82], however, calls to the witness stand), not of a marriage with a widow.

46. *Ruth R. ad* 3:11, 4:1. Also *Ruth Z.* 53; *B.B.* 91b, and others. Parenthetically, the reader will notice the Midrashic slant. It gives a positive name to "So and so," but blames not only Mahlon and Chilion for marrying Moabite women in the first place (*Mid. Ruth* ad 1:2; *B.B.* 91a . . .), but also Boaz, whom it makes die during his honeymoon with Ruth! (*Yalkut Simeoni* [thirteenth century] ad 4:13, and others). The Midrash generally has a low tolerance for subversiveness in the texts it paraphrases, be it Isaiah 53 or the book of Job. Significantly, the story of Ruth is absent from the apocrypha and pseudepigrapha, from Philo's works, and the scrolls of Qumran. Josephus (*Ant.* 5.9.318ff.) constitutes a notable exception, but he ends his report by saying that thus David was born "of such mean parents."

47. L. Levy, "Die Schuhsymbolik im jüdischen Ritus."

thus becomes clear how paradoxical and properly insulting it is when a woman removes a man's sandal. Again, here the story of Onan (whose name means virility[48]) is helpful. Calum Carmichael invites us to draw a parallel between Ruth 4 and that episode of Genesis 38.[49] When the levirate marriage is not consummated, the woman shunned by the brother-in-law symbolically imitates what happened to Tamar in her distorted relationship with Onan. She removes his sandal, that is, the male sex, and spits in his face, as he spills his semen on the ground.[50]

From here it is possible to draw some understanding of the episode of Ruth uncovering Boaz's feet on the threshing floor. Judiciously, Harold Fisch has brought together three biblical texts under the theme of "bed-trick."[51] They are Genesis 19 on Lot and his daughters, Genesis 38 on Judah and Tamar, and Ruth 3 on Ruth and Boaz. Those three narratives display striking resemblances.[52] There is first the "'Agunah-theme" (abandonment, see Ruth 1:13): "Lot's two daughters are left without the prospect of acquiring men; Tamar [is] bidden to remain a widow in her father's house; Naomi's two daughters-in-law [are] left widowed." The "bed-trick" repeats itself in the three stories. "Lot is deceived into cohabiting with his daughters, Tamar disguises herself as a prostitute, and Ruth comes secretly to the threshing-floor."

Ruth in the threshing area risks exactly the same outcome as Tamar did with Judah in Genesis 38. To provide an issue to the

48. See BDB ad loc.; K-B, s.v. *'on.*

49. Carmichael, "A Ceremonial Crux," 329.

50. *Test. of Zebulon* 3, a Midrash on Deut. 25, stresses a different but comparable symbolism. Sandals are tread under foot (v. 3). Brothers not perpetuating their brother's name put him "under foot." "Unloosing" is a sign of contempt, emphasized by the act of "spitting in his face" (v. 4). That situation can only be redeemed by providing seed to the absent one (here, Joseph, thought to be dead; v. 4). When this is not performed, the culprit(s) can expect to be metaphorically "unloosed" and humiliated ("put to shame," v. 8) by being spit upon (v. 7). See the text in *APOT* 2:329.

51. See particularly the table in H. Fisch, "Ruth and the Structure of Covenant History," 430–31.

52. M. Haller, *Ruth,* compares Ruth to Lot's daughters and to Tamar. "Three times the Old Testament conjugates the motif of the wife who, at any price, even the abandonment of her own reputation, knows how to force posterity for herself. Those are the tales of the wild daughters of Lot (Gen. 19:30-38), of Tamar (Genesis 38), and of the Moabitess Ruth" (1, my translation).

Israelite family from which she has been de jure and de facto cut off by the death of Mahlon, Ruth had gone first through the initial subversion of breaking with her family, country, gods, customs, and support structures. Then she became Naomi's substitute. Now in chapter 3 she offers her body, which, unlike Naomi's body, is fecund. This is the subversion of all standards of morality for the sake of a fidelity that transcends all other considerations. Eventually, Ruth's son Obed is Naomi's son!

Meanwhile, with her going to Boaz on the threshing floor, Ruth risks repeating Tamar's fate in almost every detail. Ruth's scheme could be exposed by a pregnancy out of wedlock, and the mother be condemned for fornication.[53] But such is not the case; there is no illegitimate pregnancy. And when Ruth conceives Obed by her husband Boaz, the latter does not refrain from "knowing her again," as in the case of Judah (Gen. 38:27).[54] Once again there occurs the redemptive recapitulation of a former biblical episode, as we saw in the case of Esther (cf. 1 Samuel 15, Saul and the Amalekite Agag), and of Judith (cf. Genesis 34, the story of Dinah). Ruth is a second Tamar—foreign, childless, widowed, transplanted within the people of Israel—who, like her model, goes to considerable lengths, indeed to prostituting herself, to obtain justice: the levirate marriage to which she is entitled. But Ruth is respected by the counterpart of Judah; she does not have to go through the shame of public denunciation and condemnation; she is willingly espoused by Boaz; her offspring is not like Perez-the-Breachmaker who ripped his mother's entrails, but is the subdued Obed-the-Servant;[55] she herself obtains an acknowledged position in Israel.

This position Ruth has won through her extraordinary attach-

---

53. On the hermeneutical sense of Genesis 38, two other texts are striking. Malachi 2:11 (ca. 465 B.C.E.) alludes to Tamar as a foreigner serving a foreign deity. One may perhaps find a similar allusion in Isa. 57:3 (end of sixth century) speaking of Israel as a "seed of an adulterer and a harlot."

54. It is true that Jewish tradition prevents this from happening by letting Boaz die on the day after the honeymoon (see note 46 above). Clearly, the halakic issue of construing Boaz's marriage as levirate but permanent proved an insurmountable dilemma. Hence, the Midrash painstakingly "proves" that it was no levirate marriage after all. Ruth 4:13 tells us that Boaz "took Ruth and she became his wife," only then "he came to her." In a levirate marriage, there is no need for a ceremony, as the woman "is married to him by Heaven," says Maimonides in *Mishneh Torah*.

55. On Obed, see also below, chapter 7 note 7.

ment to her mother-in-law.[56] Before she is faithful to her new husband, Ruth first shows *ḥesed* (steadfast love, fidelity, dedication) to another woman. Indeed, as I have insisted, she goes with her mother-in-law for Naomi's sake and with a total relinquishing of her self. By contrast, men in general appear in the book of Ruth as rather hostile or dangerous. Only a noble character like Boaz can see beyond the fact that Ruth is a Moabite and understand her courage and fidelity. The women appear as the foundational elements of society; they are also the most intuitive and open to creativity in their relations with Ruth through Naomi. They are presented as unanimously welcoming, compassionate, and sympathetic. They are moved from beginning to end by the fate of Naomi, and they are the ones who understand that Ruth means to Naomi "more than seven sons" (4:15). The hierocrats miss that point. They remain blinded by the Moabite origins of Ruth and do not see her *ḥesed,* her faithfulness, first to individual Israelites and ultimately to Israel's God. Men have become more conservative than women because of their "congealed" ideologies. In their system, there is no room for the unexpected. The institution has smothered the event.

In a way, even the best man of his generation, Boaz, must be prompted by Ruth and Naomi to surpass himself in response to the call of the extraordinary. Naomi directs her daughter-in-law to take advantage of his temporary lack of control after making merry in celebration of the harvest. Ruth is to go to him by night, uncover the lower part of his body and lie down by him (3:4). At that point Naomi is confident that the man will take over the direction of events. The scene is highly risqué; and a parallel with Judith at the camp of Holofernes could be drawn, except that Naomi and Ruth from the start trust Boaz's nobility of feelings. All the same, the situation in which Ruth places herself cannot be more compromising for her reputation, and more irreparably damaging for her purpose, if indeed she wants to be married and give progeny to her deceased husband.[57]

---

56. Phyllis Trible calls attention to the similarity of the word "to cling" in Ruth 1:14 and Gen. 2:24. Ruth clings to Naomi as man must cling to his wife; see *God and the Rhetoric of Sexuality,* 197 n. 3.

57. In this episode and elsewhere, Naomi is no "madame," to put it crudely. In Vladimir Propp's terminology (see *Morphology of the Folktale*), she is a

But, awakened by a chill upon his exposed body, the man does not take advantage of the ostensible offer of the woman. He acknowledges it as a higher degree still of Ruth's *ḥesed,* namely, dedication to her Israelite family and to her disinterested purpose.

In view of all this, I find it difficult to believe that Ruth's story could be a contemporary piece of propaganda for David and his dynasty. What kind of propaganda is this that attributes to the great king an ancestry of ill-famed mothers? There is a daughter of Lot who through incest became the mother of Moab, of whom Ruth is a descendant; the Canaanite occasional prostitute Tamar, mother of Perez through (a quasi) incest with Judah; the Canaanite professional whore Rahab, mother of Boaz. And now there is the Moabitess Ruth who goes to debatable lengths to win the favors of Boaz! One finds the same disquieting insistence on the risqué ancestresses of Jesus, descendant of David, in Matthew 1:3, 5, 6 (Tamar, Rahab, Ruth, Bathsheba) to the exclusion of any other matriarch.[58] Why would a piece of propaganda for David repeat so many times that Ruth was a Moabite or a foreigner? Why draw so close a parallel between her and Tamar?

Rather, we must set as a prerequisite for the success of Ruth's story that David be largely recognized as God-appointed. Any-

---

"dispatcher." She sets Ruth as *"hero"* on a quest, and is the ultimate beneficiary of the hero's activities. Boaz is a *"provider."* If one shifts to socioethical categories, Naomi's commission to Ruth shows once more that in Ruth woman calls man to task.

58. It is evident that the Gospel writers intended in this way to stress the *humble* origins of the Nazarene. It is quite an unheard-of kind of propaganda! Marshall D. Johnson, *The Purpose of the Biblical Genealogies with Special Reference to the Setting of the Genealogies of Jesus,* has given a full treatment (152ff.) to the Matthean introduction of the four women into Jesus' genealogy. The author points to the fact that, at the time of Matthew's composition, all of them were considered to be of Gentile stock (153). Johnson concludes that a polemic purpose prompted Matthew to include those scandalous women in Jesus' genealogy. Such a polemic, however, is already found in numerous Rabbinic texts about Davidic descent and is, therefore, internal to Judaism itself (177). In *Ruth R.* 8:1 quoted by Johnson, 169–70, for example, David is said to complain to God of his foes' slander that he is "of tainted descent . . . a descendant of Ruth the Moabitess." I would add to this that the polemic was born after the composition of the book of Ruth, but before the birth of Rabbinic Judaism. It is the book of Ruth that *created* a Moabite ancestress to David. The scandal of such claim was compounded as it became a catalyst for other notorious females, either in the alleged ancestry of David (Rahab, Tamar) or in his intimacy (Bathsheba).

one opposed to David's dynasty and to the notion of David's personal covenant with God would certainly not be convinced by Ruth as a propagandistic story. On the contrary, such an opponent would be provided with new weapons against David. On the basis of Ruth, the great king could, as a matter of fact, be considered as an alien, a mongrel, a parvenu, the outcome of unspeakable mating affairs.[59]

Apparently Goethe was somewhat blinded by his idealism when he wrote about Ruth that it "has as its noble purpose the creation of decent, interesting ancestors for a king of Israel." He added, "It can be considered as the most charming little complete piece of writing that has been handed down to us in epic and idyllic form."[60]

Much depends upon how one reads the text. Goethe thought that the book was an idyll and, following this score, an agelong tradition saw Ruth as a sweet, meek, and coy young widow, understandably intimidated by the unfamiliar surroundings in which she found herself transplanted. The truth of the matter might very well be a far cry from such a romantic image. Moab was a pastoral, seminomadic nation, where, as is typical in nomadic populations up to today in Asia and Africa, women are much freer than in rural milieus. The nomadic woman is not veiled, and she mixes freely with male company. This probably explains some features in the text of Ruth that call for attention. In 2:7, it is reported to Boaz that Ruth asked, "Let me glean and I shall tie the sheaves behind the harvesters; so she went and she has been standing from this morning until now. That [kind] takes little rest at home." It was not the custom in agrarian cultures for young women to join the team of harvesters and tie up the sheaves in payment for what they glean. Boaz's response is a remonstrance: "Cling to my maidens, you hear! . . . follow them. I order the young men not to touch you" (2:8-9). The free behavior

---

59. This is clearly the subject of the polemic referred to in the preceding note. There were milieus that expected a Messiah not of the Davidic line, or no Messiah at all (cf. Johnson, *The Purpose of the Biblical Genealogies*). A comparable anti-Cyrus polemic expressed itself in gossip that is reported by Herodotus (I.55–56.107ff.) and Xenophon (*Cyropaedia*, I.2). Cyrus's mother, it was said, was a prostitute, and she was both his mother and his wife.

60. Goethe, in *Göthe's Werke*, 21:231; quoted and translated in *The Hebrew Bible in Literary Criticism*, 3.

of the widow seems to have created some frivolous reactions among the males, for Boaz's recommendations to them are twice repeated, in 2:15 and 2:16b.

Ruth goes through all this untroubled. In her report to Naomi, she tells her, "He—that is Boaz—even told me, 'Cling to my young men, until they completely finish my harvest'" (2:21), a statement that Naomi corrects with the words, "It is better, my daughter, that you go out with his maidens!" (2:22). It is clear that if the young woman does not understand all the nuances of the relations between the sexes in a sedentary society, the cause is her Moabite origins. Each time she blunders, the text reminds us that she is a foreigner. It is "Ruth the Moabitess" who reports to Naomi about Boaz's permission to stay with the workers. Earlier, when Boaz was inquiring about that strange young woman among the harvesters with the revealing question, "To whom belongs that young person?" he received the answer, "She's a Moabite girl."[61] The response is significant. It does not answer the question, except by indirection. She belongs to no one, but comes from a strange place where such questions are inappropriate.

Ruth's sociological and ethnological peculiarity does not, however, remain at the idiosyncratic level. Robert Alter has shown that in the story of Ruth, "the author has rotated the betrothal type-scene 180 degrees on the axes of gender and geography. The protagonist is a heroine, not a hero, and her homeland is Moab, so the 'foreign soil' on which she meets her future mate near a well is Judaea." Fitting such a reversal of the traditional elements of the betrothal scene, here it is the young men who draw water for Ruth to drink (2:9).[62]

Furthermore, another "rotation" must be noticed, this time along an existential axis. There is in Ruth's stance a transformation of Abraham's act of faith. In the words of Phyllis Trible,

> By comparison, not even Abraham's leap of faith is greater. Whereas YHWH chooses Abraham, Ruth herself chooses YHWH. Ruth lives without promise. Prospects for blessing are not only

---

61. Note the irreverent and even downright contemptuous *zeh* ("that") to designate Ruth in 2:7. This ethnological aspect of the story of Ruth has been keenly noticed by P. Crapon de Caprona, *Ruth la Moabite.*

62. Alter, *Art of Biblical Narrative,* 58.

discounted; they are denied. Naomi has no other son to become the husband of Ruth. The God whom Ruth chooses to serve turns sweetness into bitterness, fullness into emptiness (1:20-21).[63]

What a contrast with the Jerusalem hierocrats, whose "clinging" is to their privileges as chosen people. Implicitly in Ruth, they are scolded for refusing to make the leap of faith exemplified by Ruth and Abraham.

Through contrasted parallels with the betrothal type-scene and with Abraham's uprooting, in addition to its multiple references to other women of the Bible, the book of Ruth, to be sure, strikes roots in the *Heilsgeschichte* of Israel. But the reversals in question are far-reaching. They are best appreciated within the broader context of a shift imposed by the author from male perspective to female perspective. Contemporary female critics have been particularly sensitive to this point. Trible observes that Ruth 1:1 refers to "his wife," but that the story soon speaks of "her husband" (1:3), and switches from "his two sons" to "her two sons." The two foreign daughters-in-law, rather surprisingly, are sent back to their mother's houses (1:8).[64] To this, Adele Berlin adds that the story is focused from Naomi's vantage point. All characters are set in reference to her, although Ruth is the center of interest. The Moabite climbs the social scale step by step. First, she calls herself a "foreigner" (2:10), then a "maidservant" (2:13) and a "handservant" (3:9). But, eventually, she becomes "the wife who enters your house" (4:11). Boaz calls her also in a progressive order, a "young woman" (2:5), then "my daughter" (3:11a), and finally "a worthy woman" (3:11b), like himself, who is "a man of worth" (2:1).[65] Samuel Sandmel wonders whether perhaps Ruth's author was a woman.[66] The question seems to me legitimate but impossible to answer with any certainty; as we have seen, the author is so skillful that he or she

63. Trible, "Depatriarchalizing in Biblical Interpretation." See Ruth 1:17, 2:11-12.

64. Trible, *Rhetoric*, 169–70.

65. A. Berlin, *Poetics and Interpretation of Biblical Narrative*, 84ff. Cf. Trible, *Rhetoric*, 184: "Female and male; foreigner and native; youth and age; poor and wealthy—all these opposites are mediated by human worth."

66. S. Sandmel, *The Enjoyment of Scripture*, 25.

tailors style and vocabulary to fit the age and gender of the one who speaks.

Be that as it may, even the principal male character in the story, Boaz, does not step onto the center stage. His intervening is obviously indispensable, but the narrative does not allow the feminine complex Naomi/Ruth to be sidetracked. This the Jewish Midrash has keenly felt. It says that Boaz died on the day after the wedding![67] Whether or not he died, the story does not linger on the happiness of the newlyweds. It immediately and factually lets us know that Ruth conceived, thanks to YHWH, and bore a son (4:13). The denouement, according to the received text *(textus receptus)* develops into a genealogy that indicates the providential course of the reported events: upon the union of Ruth and Boaz depended the coming of King David.

There is a quasi consensus among scholars to dismiss the final genealogy as a later addition to the book. The genealogical taxonomy seems so different from the narrative genre that it is, of course, impossible to decide on its own merit whether it was composed by the author of the tale. Generally speaking, critics tend to suspect the authenticity of the context of all genealogies, with the exception of the Priestly source and the Chronicler's work. In the book of Ruth, however, it must be noted that the genealogical motif, culminating as it does with the advent of King David, corresponds perfectly with the mention at the beginning of the story of Bethlehem, the home city of King David,[68] contrary opinions by O. Eissfeldt, G. Fohrer, and others notwithstanding. Eissfeldt writes, "the Ruth narrative had originally nothing at all to do with David, but has only secondarily been made into a narrative concerning David's ancestors."[69] This statement is all the more surprising when we realize that 2 Sam. 15:18-22 demonstrates that Ruth's author intentionally modeled

---

67. *Ruth Z.* 55; *Lekah Ruth* 4.17. See note 46 above.
68. See 1 Sam. 17:12,15; 20:6,28. David was anointed there by Samuel, 1 Sam. 16:1-13. In Ruth, there are seven mentions of Bethlehem: 1:1-2,19,22; 2:4; 4:11. In contrast, "field(s) of Moab" occurs six times (1:2,22; 1:6; 2:6; 4:3).
69. O. Eissfeldt, *The Old Testament: An Introduction,* 480. Cf. G. Fohrer, *Introduction to the Old Testament,* 251, and the reaction of Louise Pettibone-Smith in *Interpreter's Bible* 2:831.

the beginning of the story on Ittai the foreigner, who decided to cling to David in a time of crisis when he was invited to return to "his place." See especially v. 21.

This is not the place to get into a discussion of biblical genealogies, one of whose functions is to provide a kind of historical summary (and therefore genealogies are not foreign to narrative genre). A few remarks, however, are appropriate. The genealogy at the end of Ruth (4:18-22) is carefully built. It is repeated almost verbatim in Matt. 1:3-6, and, earlier, it is found in 1 Chron. 2:10-17. Its contents are characterized by contraction. With the increase of the chronological distance between the facts and their reporting, the genealogical lines become shorter and kinship relations are simplified. The taxonomic mention of the most important names at key places belongs to this systematization process. In Ruth 4:18-22, Tamar's son Perez is in the first position, Boaz in the seventh, and David in the tenth. This so perfectly suits the tale of Ruth that one must conclude to an ad hoc composition of the genealogy. Consequently, the question of authorship or of "authenticity" becomes almost irrelevant.[70]

As the genealogy now stands, at the end of the story—a very unusual occurrence—its function is clearly to link Ruth to the main narrative sequence that runs from Genesis to Kings. As Jack Sasson writes, *"the genealogy of 4:18-22 actually begins the tale of Obed, rather than ends that of Boaz!"*[71]

Obed is twice the child of miracle. First, he is born from the improbable union of a Moabitess and an older Israelite. Moreover, the text that reports his birth says, "He went in to her but YHWH gave her conception," clearly in fulfillment of the blessing twice uttered by Boaz in 2:12 and 3:10. Now YHWH has broken up the tragic circle of death, famine, and emptiness in which Naomi was suffocating at the beginning of the story (1:20-21).

Furthermore, the formula of 4:13b is an echo of a recurring biblical statement about the birth of children of the promise.

70. B. Porten emphasizes the "concentric structure" of Ruth, and he sees in the birth of ten generations in Israel as reported by Ruth 4:18-22 the antitype of the ten years of death in Moab of Ruth 1:1-6; see *Beth Mikra*, 224–25; quoted and translated in *The Hebrew Bible in Literary Criticism*, 544.

71. J. Sasson, *Ruth: A New Translation with a Philological Commentary and a Formalist-Folklorist Interpretation*, 213.

Philo, in particular, already in the first century c.e. called attention to that textual particularity. The children of the divine promise are children of miracle.[72] The line starts, of course, with the birth of Isaac from parents too old to beget children. It continues with the birth of Jacob from a sterile woman, Rebekah. With the third son of the promise, the text becomes even more insistent. Rachel begs her husband Jacob, "Give me children, or I die" (Gen. 30:1), to which plea Jacob prophetically answers, "Am I in God's stead?" (Gen. 30:2), for only God can open the womb of Rachel. She gives birth to Joseph, acknowledging, "God has taken away my shame" (Gen. 30:23). The line continues with Moses, Samuel, David, Solomon . . . Emmanuel, and the Gospel insists on the miraculous birth of the Messiah, ultimate offspring of a line that started with the origins of Israel.

Obed clearly has his place in that line. He is begotten by a saintly Israelite man and an extraordinary Moabite widow. However, these parents are not "really" the begetters, for the child is God's. In the human lineage also his status is paradoxical. He is "the son of Naomi," that tragic figure of Israelite widowhood and childlessness.[73] She is "restored" so that a name in Israel will not be blotted out. There is something misleading in Trible's conclusion that the women of Bethlehem

> perceive this infant as restoring life to the living rather than restoring a name to the dead. They speak of Ruth the bearer rather than of Boaz the begetter. And they themselves name the baby. Repeatedly, these women stand as opposites to the elders.[74]

Phyllis Trible has transposed a modern problematic into a Second Temple period story. She sees in the text the war between the sexes, while the opposition here is not between males and females per se, but between what they represent in the conflict between ideologists and utopians in Jerusalem. The "elders" are

72. See *On the Cherubim,* xii–xiv.

73. Ruth as mother of Obed is considered at that moment by the fiction of the tale as if she had been a kind of servant (cf. 2:13; 3:9) that Naomi offered to Boaz for the procreation of a child who would legally belong to the "infertile" woman. It is another fiction to have Naomi play the role of the childless woman when in fact she bore two sons who are dead at that time. See E. Lipiński, "Le mariage de Ruth."

74. Trible, *Rhetoric,* 194.

not opposed because they wear a beard but because they shore up the establishment. The institution, ever since Ezra-Nehemiah, has ostracized all foreign women from Israel's community. It was to be expected that the literature of opposition put in the fore feminine figures that set examples for all to emulate.

Until now, I have left untouched the question of name symbolism in the book of Ruth. With the final genealogy, however, such a problem cannot be further delayed. I have shown elsewhere that the proper names in the story are without parallel in the Scriptures and belong to the symbolism of the book, like the uncovering of the feet, or the removal of the sandal.[75] Ruth 1:20 invites the reader to be aware of that key for the understanding of the tale. "Do not call me Naomi, call me Mara, for Shaddai has dealt very bitterly with me." A. Graeme Auld writes, "Some of [the names] at least are chosen to illustrate the characteristics of the actors or the drama."[76] In fact, all of the names in Ruth are illustrative, but here again, as the book was ostensibly set in the time of Judges, modern exegetes felt that they could not cross those time limits in their quest for the meaning of the names. The critics thus blocked the very door leading to solution. As we shall see, what rescued the Talmud from that self-condemnation of sorts was its hermeneutical principle that chronology is not decisive in exegesis.

The scope of this essay does not allow for a review of all the names in the Ruth story. I shall confine myself to those of the two heroines, Naomi and Ruth. "Naomi" is an unusual female name. In fact, it appears under this form only here (twenty times in the book of Ruth). Naamah, however, which is the same word in Hebrew, was the sister of Tubal-cain (Gen. 4:22), and, more interestingly for us, the Ammonite wife of Solomon, mother of the future king Rehoboam. This Naamah of 1 Kings 14:21, 31 most probably served as a model for the author of Ruth (note the emphasis on the nationality of Rehoboam's mother there and also in 2 Chron. 12:13). In Ruth, Naamah the Ammonite becomes, by chiatic reuse, Naomi the Israelite (accompanied by the Moabite Ruth).[77]

Naamah is a descendant of one of Lot's two daughters (Gen. 19:36-38), as Ruth is a descendant of the other. So, in the book of Ruth, Ammon and Moab are joined together with Israel again. The fracture healed brings about a redeemed offspring. Naamah mothered the weak Rehoboam, under whose reign idolatry was rampant in Judah (1 Kings 14:24) and the Temple was profaned. Conversely, from the conjunction of the Ephratite Naomi/Boaz and the Moabite Ruth (on the model of Solomon and Naamah), are born Obed and eventually David, the founder of the Temple.[78] The lesson to the Temple-based ideologists in Jerusalem could not be clearer.

"Ruth" is hardly an abbreviation of the form *Re'uth* (female companion), which is used in the Syriac text of Ruth. No one is satisfied with that linguistic association or derivation,[79] but it is the one that most exegetes stubbornly propose.[80] Ruth as a name appears only here, some twelve times. Philologically it has nothing to do with *r'h* (to be companion), but with *rwh* (to water to saturation), a derivation of which the Talmud is keenly aware. *Baba Bathra* 14b says, "Rabbi Yochanan said, Why was she called Ruth? Because there issued from her David who saturated the Holy One, blessed be He, with songs and praises." In another text, *Berakhot* 7b, we read, Ruth "was privileged as from her descended David who saturated the Holy One, etc."[81]

But, if so, what is the metaphorical meaning of the name "Ruth"? The figurative use of the root *rwh* in Scriptures is illumi-

---

77. Astutely, Jewish tradition associates Ruth the Moabitess and Naamah the Ammonitess, wife of Solomon. See *Gen. R. 50. Yebam.* 63a reads, ". . . The Holy One, blessed be He, said to Araham, I have two goodly shoots to engraft on you: Ruth the Moabitess and Naamah the Ammonitess" (quoted by M. Johnson, *The Purpose of the Biblical Genealogies,* 169).

78. The name *Boaz* is in reference to the Temple. It designates the left (northern) pillar at the entrance of the Temple built by Hiram of Tyre (1 Kings 7:15-22).

79. See K-B, ad loc.

80. Even Humbert, *Opuscules,* 85.

81. H. Bruppacher must be credited with the adoption of this etymology; see "Die Bedeutung des Namens Ruth."

nating. Jeremiah 31:12-14 speaks of the return from exile. Israel then shall be satiated with every good and with the Lord's goodness. Isaiah 58:11 describes in terms of *rwh* the eschatological fulfillment of exile oracles. In mythopoeic language, Jer. 46:10 speaks eschatologically of the sword of Y<small>HWH</small> "satiated" with the blood of his enemies. A parallel is provided in the sixth century by Isa. 34:5-7.

In other words, the name "Ruth" makes clear the role of the nations in the restoration and, beyond, in the advent of the eschatological messianic era. As "Mahlon" ("sickness") was the disease *(mahlah)* that hit the Egyptians before the Exodus (Exod. 15:26); and as "Chilion" was an "emptying out" and metaphorically a sign of dispersion through exile, "Ruth" is the filling up to saturation, metaphorically a sign of restoration and redemption—she, a Moabitess!

CHAPTER 7

Conclusion

Susanna, Judith, Esther, Ruth—four heroines gave their
names to books produced in the midst of a patriarchally oriented
literature. Each of these books anthologically reflects on feminine
characters and feats of women from the origins of tradition,
running from Sarah to Rebekah, to Tamar, to Bathsheba. . . .
Susanna, Judith, Esther, and Ruth display innocence, courage,
leadership, and self-forgetfulness, respectively. They are four
women who break the stereotypes of femininity, not by becoming
masculine, but by transcending the male-female polarity while
remaining the "feminine" females that they are.

An element common to all of them is their sharp criticism of
an ideology[1] incapable of generosity and of real sensitivity, as it
understands its task as one of compartmentalizing and categoriz-
ing the ethical rules of an exclusivistic community. As subversive
literature, the four books that we have reviewed feature a child
wiser than the elders, and a woman purer than the "specialists" in
legal purity. They present a widow single-handedly defeating the
most powerful dictator of antiquity. Another young Jewess saves
her people from genocide and, in the process of redemption, she
humanizes the whole Persian Empire. Finally, a young Moabi-

1. According to P. Ricoeur (in a personal communication), "ideology" never
recognizes itself as such (one exception is communism in the USSR). It is only
others who use the term accusingly in reference to the party they oppose.
Among the criticisms of ideology are its alleged global notion of the world and
its twisted use of discourse, which has switched from persuasion to seduction.

117

tess becomes the golden link in the generational chain of *Heilsge-schichte.* She is the genetrix of the messianic line.

All those improbable characters are intimately related with Israel, their people, either by birth or by adoption. Although ostensibly separated by belonging to vastly different epochs— from the time of Judges to the era of the Persian Empire—they can be envisaged synchronically as rescuing their community from moral bankruptcy or from physical annihilation, two threats of equal import in Israel's conception. All four are living demonstrations of the ineptitude of institutionalized answers to adversity. As circumstances rarely remain "normal" for long, they soon become extraordinary and demand extraordinary responses. At that point, the inspiration coming from the establishment remains desperately wanting. Where the "institution" fails, the "event" must take its place. It is then made clear that God opts for the unexpected, the unconventional, even the extravagant; first in the choice of his agents, then in the choice of means by which these will bring about Israel's liberation. The Israelite tradition keeps alive the remembrance of those characters and their deeds, because it is conscious of the blessedness for any generation of having such willing instruments of God's saving acts. Keeping their memory alive thus becomes a prayer that there will always be servants of the Lord ready synergetically to make real God's kingship over history.

This applies to the whole of history, not just Israel's destiny. The representative function of the four heroines makes them not just paradigms for Israel, but symbols for all humanity of the triumph of the Spirit.

As we have seen, something belonging to what could be called their style brings these women together, namely, the salvation of their people by *substitutional self-offering.* Judith adorns herself as a sacrificial victim. "Judith's great beauty invites assault," said Toni Craven;[2] the altar on which she is willing to be offered is Holofernes' tent. Esther goes uninvited to face her terrible husband, the Persian "Bluebeard" Ahasuerus, and she reveals to him that she belongs to the condemned people. If the royal rage

2. Craven, *Artistry and Faith.*

erupts, Esther will deliberately become the lightning rod and be consumed in the process. Ruth is the epitome of abnegation. She surrogates herself to her mother-in-law in order to save an Israelite line from extinction, although she herself is a Moabitess. Veritable redeemer of an Israelite clan, her self-sacrifice is eventually revealed for what it is: a national salvation. The Moabitess is a vital link in the convenantal history between God and his people. She happens to give to *Heilsgeschichte* its last and supreme push, one that promotes it to the rank of messianic achievements.

In all of the stories there is a happy ending. These tales belong to comedy—but not to farce. Justice, or peace, or hope, are restored only after much suffering and terrible threats. It is only after sowing in tears that the harvest comes with songs of joy (cf. Ps. 126:5). Between the trials and their happy resolution, the narrative uses a literary device with which Greek rhetoric has familiarized us: *peripeteia.*[3] According to Israel—or should we say, according to Jewish postexilic thinking?—that sudden turn of fortune reflects most appropriately the divine lordship over history. Psalm 126 precisely starts by mentioning peripety, not as a literary device, however, but as a theological statement: "When the Lord turned the tide of Zion's fortune."[4] The psalm's language, referring as it does to the liberation from exile in Babylon, is very close to the *shub-shebuth* formula of the prophets of exile, Jeremiah and Ezekiel. The expression means amphibologically the freedom of captives, and the turn of fortune. For Jeremiah and Ezekiel this act of salvation amounts to theophany, creation, and redemption.

In the postexilic era, peripety in history is the catalyst of the community's (or communities') hope. On the model of the "turning of the tide of Zion's fortune" in 538 B.C.E., God will again show his redeeming care and power toward his people in the future. Thus, a child vindicates justice when it had been flouted by elders. The intended victim triumphs and is praised by all. A widow demonstrates that God's power comes to its full strength

3. See Aristotle, *Poetics,* chap. 11, 1452A 21ff.
4. Psalm 126:1, New English Bible.

in weakness (cf. 2 Cor. 12:9). She changes despair into festival. So does another woman, a Jewess in the eastern Diaspora. Her people's murder and plunder was decided, edicted, dated. But, in the image of her God—even though he remains unmentioned— Esther "changes seasons and times" (cf. Dan. 2:21). In a gamelike ironic reversal of situation, those who fall victims of wickedness are not the intended innocents, but the guilty party of "Amalekites." Haman the wicked, his sons, and his supporters are chastized; and the Jews of Persia celebrate Purim.

As usual in Hebrew literature, the form befits the contents. It is remarkable indeed how the redeeming substitution at the hingepoint of the plot is echoed at every level of the composition, in the image of the running ripples on the surface of a pond. (Even Haman, Holofernes, and the licentious elders are substitute victims, but with a negative meaning. They are the foil of the one "who made [herself] himself a sacrifice for sin" [Isa. 53:10].) In the book of Ruth in particular, swapping occurs at every level of the text. Ruth surrogates herself to Naomi, Boaz to "So and so," Naomi to Ruth, Obed to Boaz.... The whole story is conditioned by the principles of surrogation at the basis of the levirate marriage. In Susanna, the child Daniel replaces the elders. Judith also substitutes herself for Bethulia officials; Bethulia for Jerusalem; and Achior for the "nations" (more specifically the medley of peoples drafted by Nebuchadnezzar).

At a deeper level yet, there is also surrogation of texts to texts. In the background of Judith is Genesis 34, the story of Dinah raped by "the Shechemites" and avenged by her brothers Simeon and Levi through deceit and massacre. Jacob then not only refuses to condone such a deed, but, on his deathbed, his sons' benediction becomes, as regards Simeon and Levi, very ambiguous, if not an outright curse (see Gen. 49:5-7). Judith is at once Dinah, Simeon, and Levi. Like Dinah, she is exposed to rape; she is a descendant of Simeon;[5] and she replaces the levitic priestly cadres of Bethulia. As a Simeonite, she also uses wiles and deceit, but this time the deceptor is no warrior but a helpless widow. And the deceived are no ambiguous allies; they are unequivocally

---

5. As Mordecai is a descendant of Saul, and Haman a descendant of Agag.

the enemies of her people. Holofernes the uncircumcised is a second Goliath. Like him, he will be beheaded by a "weakling." In addition, the rape of Judith/Dinah is this time not consummated; and the population of Bethulia can celebrate without ambivalence the victory of "Dinah" over her aggressors. The story of Ruth recapitulates the tragic failure of the first encounter of Moab and Israel in the "plains of Moab" (Numbers 22ff.). This time—which is an entirely new opportunity, as when Jonah 3:1 says "a second time"—the meeting requires the leaving behind of "the plains of Moab" (Ruth 1:22): it occurs on Israel's ground. The corruption of the exiles from Egypt by Moabite females is now redeemed by Ruth's *hesed* toward Israel and her God. The Moabite femininity is no longer used for wantonness, but for the perpetuation of an Israelite line that leads to the great King David, and, beyond, to the Messiah.[6]

Judith is another Dinah; Ruth is another Tamar. Like Tamar the Canaanite, Ruth the Moabite shrinks from nothing to see that justice be done *in Israel*. She is ready to go through the shame of prostitution and public denunciation. But, as in the Judith story, the events are transfigured. Ruth does not hide herself under the veil of a prostitute. She does not entice Boaz, although she displays a total vulnerability. Unlike his predecessor Judah, Boaz does not take advantage of circumstances. Intercourse out of wedlock does not occur. Ruth's pregnancy will be legitimate, and her marriage with Boaz a true marriage. While Perez "ripped" the body of his mother, Obed is obedient;[7] that is what the names

6. Thus 1 Sam. 22:3-4, which deals with David's relationships with Moab, becomes a mysterious promise, hardly formulated, that would dissolve like a *hebel* (a breath, a vanity) without Ruth. The Deuteronomic historian probably had no idea of the prophetic dimension of his brief notice in 1 Samuel; but the author of Ruth uncovers that dimension and brings the message to its accomplishment by giving to David a Moabite ancestress. A hermeneutical reflection is here possible on "authorial intention," for example, or on the open-endedness of texts that must be *reread* in the light of subsequent developments that are also embodied in texts. The Hebrew Scripture provides us with multiple examples of intertextuality, and thus of a self-referential hermeneutics.

7. The pun is intended! It is interesting to note that the name Obed, frequent after Ruth (mentioned in 1 Chron. 2:12,37f.; 11:47) occurs here for the first time. If it is traceable back to Obed-Edom of 2 Sam. 6:10-12 (cf. 1 Chron. 13:13f.; 15:25), then there is in the child's name a clear allusion to Edom, as there is a possible allusion to Ammon in the name Naomi (the same name,

of these two physically and mysteriously related children indicate. A stronger tie, of course, binds them together: Obed is a descendant of Perez, and both are ancestors of David. It was unfitting that King David and the Messiah be born from Perez, "The Maker of Breaches," prior to his antitype, Obed, "The Obedient." Paradoxically, it is the Moabitess who brings about the miracle.

Finally, Esther is the successful recapitulation of another somber page in Israel's history, one that is reported in 1 Samuel 15. It is again the story of a confrontation with a foreign nation, Amalek. As can be expected, there is in Esther no redemption of Amalek. Ammon is "recuperable" in the person of Achior, Moab in Ruth's, but Amalek has become in Israelite tradition the epitome of enmity and wickedness. Between Israel and Amalek the war is to the death. Saul missed the point in a most disastrous way. He thought that there was a possibility of mediation between good and evil, yea and nay, light and darkness, the Messiah and Hitler. It cost Saul his kingship. His miscalculation yielded bitter fruits much beyond "the third and fourth generations," even to the time of the Iranian dispersion of the Jewish people. Haman is a descendant of Agag, king of Amalek, whom Saul spared. Mordecai is a descendant of Saul; he is determined not to repeat the blunder of his ancestor. Between the mongoose and the serpent the fight is to the finish. When Haman hangs on the gallows that he erected for Mordecai, 1 Samuel 15 can be put to rest, as it were. The event has reached its fulfillment. A whole section of history enters the "Sabbath" of accomplishment. The Jews call Sabbath a queen. Queen Esther and Queen Sabbath are related; one introduces the other. It is not accidental if Esther is also the queen of the festival of Purim, when "the Jews found repose from their enemies" (Esth. 9:22).

At the end of our inquiry, one is moved by the pleasant feeling that the balance has been struck by the Hebrew literature of

with a slight change in the spelling, as Naamah, the Ammonite wife of Solomon; cf. 1 Kings 14:21,31; note the emphasis on the nationality of Rehoboam's mother; see also 2 Chron. 12:13). When we include the Moabite background of Ruth, the trilogy of nations in the book is impressive.

subversion, making women decisive factors of the ongoing *Heils-geschichte.* If any text is redeemed, beyond Numbers 22ff., Genesis 34 and 38, and 1 Samuel 15, it is Ezra 10. Divorcing foreign wives and sending away the children born from those marriages (v. 3) could not remain without a lashing protest. Then was constituted a "Pentateuch" of women: Ruth, Song of Songs,[8] Esther, Judith, Susanna. With those women, Israelite religion emerged from a one-sided patriarchal mold. The times were ripe for the collective Woman to give birth to Emmanuel.

8. I intend to propose a study of the Song of Songs in a forthcoming publication, emphasizing its subversive nature.

Bibliography

Adler, R., and Seligson, M. *Une nouvelle chronique samaritaine.* Paris, 1903.

Alonso-Schökel, L. "Narrative Structures in the Book of Judith." *Protocol Series of the Colloquies of the Center for Hermeneutical Studies in Hellenistic and Modern Culture.* Vol. 11, no. 17. Berkeley, 1975, 1–20.

Alter, R. *The Art of Biblical Narrative.* New York: Harper & Row, 1981.

Auerbach, E. "Figura." *Scenes from the Drama of European Literature,* 11–76. New York: Meridian Books, 1959.

Auld, A. G. *Ruth.* Philadelphia: Westminster Press, 1984.

Bal, M. *Lethal Love: Feminist Literary Readings of Biblical Love Stories.* Bloomington, Ind.: Indiana University Press, 1987.

Baldwin, J. G. *Esther.* Tyndale Old Testament Commentaries. London, 1984.

Beattie, D. R. G. "The Book of Ruth as Evidence for Israel's Legal Practice." *VT* 24 (1974): 251–67.

Bennett, E. K. *A History of the German Novelle from Göthe to Thomas Mann.* Cambridge: At the University Press, 1934.

Benveniste, E. *Problèmes de linguistique générale.* Paris: Gallimard, 1966.

Berg, S. B. *The Book of Esther: Motifs, Themes and Structure.* Missoula, Mont.: Scholars Press, 1979.

Berlin, A. *Poetics and Interpretation of Biblical Narrative.* Sheffield: JSOT Press, 1983.

Beyerlin, W., editor. *Near Eastern Religious Texts Relating to the Old Testament.* Philadelphia: Westminster Press, 1978 (1975).

Bickerman, E. "The Colophon of the Greek Book of Esther." *JBL* 63 (1944): 339–62.

———. "Notes on the Greek Book of Esther." *Proceedings of the American Academy for Jewish Research* 20 (1950): 101–33.

———. *Four Strange Books of the Bible.* New York: Schocken, 1984 (1967).

———. *The Jews in the Greek Age.* Cambridge, Mass.: Harvard University Press, 1988.

Bornkamm, H. *Luther and the Old Testament.* Philadelphia: Fortress Press, 1969.

Brüll, N. "Das apokryphische Susanna Buch." *JJGL* 3 (1877): 1–69.

Bruppacher, H. "Die Bedeutung des Namens Ruth." *TZ* 22 (1966): 12–18.

Campbell, E. F. "The Hebrew Short Story: A Study of Ruth." In *A Light unto My Path.* Philadelphia: Temple University Press, 1974, 83–101.

———. *Ruth.* AB 7. Garden City, N.Y.: Doubleday, 1975.

Carmichael, C. M. "A Ceremonial Crux: Removing a Man's Sandal as a Female Gesture of Contempt." *JBL* 96/3 (1977): 321–36.

Cazelles, H. "Note sur la composition du rouleau d'Esther." *Lex tua veritas* (FS Hubert Junker), edited by H. Gross and F. Mussner. Trier, West Germany: Paulinus Vlg., 1961.

Charles, R. H., editor. *Apocrypha and Pseudepigrapha of the Old Testament.* Two volumes. Oxford: Clarendon, 1913.

Clines, D. J. A. *The Esther Scroll: The Story of the Story.* Sheffield: JSOT Press, 1984.

———. "Ezra, Nehemiah, Esther." *The New Century Bible Commentary.* Grand Rapids: Eerdmans, 1982.

Coates, G. W., editor. *Saga, Legend, Tale, Novella, Fable: Narrative Form in Old Testament Literature.* Sheffield: JSOT Press, 1985.

Cohen, A. D. "Hu Ha-Goral: The Religious Significance of Esther." *Judaism* 89 (1974): 87–94.

Cohen, S. J. D. *From the Maccabees to the Mishnah*. Philadelphia: Westminster Press, 1987.

Corpus Scriptorum Historiae Byzantinae. Volume 6. Bonn: E. Weber, 1829.

Crable, R. *Using Communication*. Boston: Allyn, 1979.

Craghan, J. F. "Esther, Judith, and Ruth: Paradigms for Human Liberation." *BTB* 12 (1982): 11–19.

Crapon de Caprona, P. *Ruth la Moabite*. Geneva: Labor et Fides, 1982.

Craven, T. "Artistry and Faith in the Book of Judith." *Semeia* 8 (1977): 75–101.

————. *Artistry and Faith in the Book of Judith*. Atlanta: Scholars Press, 1983.

Dancy, J. C., editor. *The Shorter Books of the Apocrypha*. Cambridge: Cambridge University Press, 1972.

Daube, D. "The Last Chapter of Esther." *JQR* 37 (1946–47): 139–47.

DiLella, A. A. See Hartman, L. F.

Durant, W. *The Story of Civilization*. Volume 2. New York: Simon and Schuster, 1935.

Eissfeldt, O. *The Old Testament: An Introduction*. New York: Harper and Row, 1965.

Eliade, M. *A History of Religious Ideas*. Volume 1. Chicago: University of Chicago Press, 1978.

Fichman, J. '*Arugot*. Jerusalem: Bialik Institute, 1954, 282–86.

Fisch, H. "Ruth and the Structure of Covenant History." *VT* 32/4 (1982): 425–37.

Flusser, D., editor. *Sefer Yosippon*. Volume 1. Jerusalem: Bialik Institute, 1981.

Fohrer, G. *Introduction to the Old Testament*. Nashville: Abingdon Press, 1968.

Fox, M. "The Structure of the Book of Esther." In *Isac Leo Seeligmann Volume,* edited by A. Rofé and Y. Zakovitch. Jerusalem: E. Rubinstein's Publ. House, 1983, 291–303.

Gaster, M., editor. *Chronicles of Jerahmeel*. London: Royal Asiatic Society, 1899.

Gaster, T. *Purim and Hanukkah in Custom and Tradition*. New York: Schuman, 1950.

Gerleman, G. "Studien zu Esther: Stoff-Struktur-Stil-Sinn." *Biblische Studien* 48 (1966): 1–48.

———. *Esther.* Biblischer Kommentar 21. Neukirchen-Vluyn: Neukirchener, 1973.

Ginzberg, L. *The Legends of the Jews.* Volume 2, "Joseph"; Volume 4, "Esther." Philadelphia: The Jewish Publication Society, 1954.

Giraudoux, Jean. *Judith, Tragédie en 3 actes.* Paris: Grasset, 1932.

Glueck, N. *Das Wort Häsäd.* BZAW. Berlin: Alf. Töpelmann, 1927. In Engl. transl.: *Hesed in the Bible.* Cincinnati: Hebrew Union College Press, 1967.

Goethe, J. W. von. *West-östlicher Divan.* In *Göthe's Werke,* volume 21. Vienna and Stuttgart, 1820.

Goitein, S. D. *Iyyunim ba-Mikra.* Studies in Scriptures. Tel Aviv: Yavneh Press, 1957.

———. "Women as Creators of Biblical Genres." *Prooftexts* 8 (1988): 1–33.

Gordis, R. "Love, Marriage, and Business in the Book of Ruth." In *A Light unto My Path* (FS J. M. Myers). Philadelphia: Temple University Press, 1974, 241–64.

———. "Religion, Wisdom and History in the Book of Esther: A New Solution to an Ancient Crux," *JBL* 100 (1981): 359–88.

Gottwald, N. *The Tribes of Yahweh.* Maryknoll, N.Y.: Orbis, 1979.

Gray, J. *Joshua, Judges and Ruth.* The New Century Bible. Grand Rapids: Eerdmans, 1967.

Greenstein, E. L. "A Jewish Reading of Esther." In *Judaic Perspectives on Ancient Israel,* edited by J. Neusner, B. A. Levine, and E. S. Frerichs. Philadelphia: Fortress Press, 1987.

Grintz, Y. M. *The Book of Judith* (Hebrew). Jerusalem: Bialik Institute, 1957.

Gunkel, H. *Reden und Aufsätze.* Göttingen, 1913.

Gutierrez, G. *Hablar de Dios desde el sufrimiento del inocente: Una reflexion sobre el libro de Job.* Lima, 1986. In English: *On Job.* Maryknoll, N.Y.: Orbis, 1987.

Hadas, M. *Hellenistic Culture: Fusion and Diffusion.* New York: Norton, 1959.

Haller, M. *Esther.* HAT 1/18. Tübingen: Mohr, 1940.

————. *Ruth.* HAT 1/18. Tübingen: Mohr, 1940.

Hals, R. M. *The Theology of the Book of Ruth.* Philadelphia: Fortress Press, 1969.

————. "Ruth, Book of." *IDB Supp.,* 758–59.

Hartman, L. F., and DiLella, A. A. *The Book of Daniel.* AB 23. Garden City, N.Y.: Doubleday, 1978.

Harvey, D. "Book of Ruth." *IDB* 4: 131–34.

Hengel, M. *Judaism and Hellenism.* Two volumes. Philadelphia: Fortress Press, 1971.

Hoenig, S. B. "Bel and the Dragon." *IDB* 1: 376–77.

————. "Susanna." *IDB* 4: 467–68.

Holladay, W. L. "Jeremiah XXVI 22b reconsidered: 'The Woman encompasses the man,'" *VT* 16 (1966): 236–39.

Huet, G. "Daniel et Susanne: Note de littérature comparée." *RHR* 65 (1912): 277–84.

————. "Daniel et Suzanne." *RHR* 76 (1917): 129–30.

Humbert, P. *Opuscules d'un hébraïsant.* Neuchatel: Université de Neuchâtel, 1958.

Humphreys, W. L. "The Story of Esther and Mordecai: An Early Jewish Novella." See Coates, G. W., editor.

James, Henry. *The Turn of the Screw.* New York: W. W. Norton, 1966.

Jensen, P. "Elamitische Eigennamen. Ein Beitrag zur Erklärung der elamitischen Inschriften." *WZKM* 6 (1892), 47–70, 209–26.

Jones, B. W. "Two Misconceptions about the Book of Esther." *CBQ* 39 (1977): 171–81.

Johnson, M. *The Purpose of the Biblical Genealogies with Special Reference to the Setting of the Genealogies of Jesus.* 2nd ed. Cambridge: At the University Press, 1988.

Kamlah, E. "Susanna." *Biblisch-Historisches Handwörterbuch.* Volume 3, 1896.

Kautzsch, E., editor. *Die Apokryphen und Pseudepigraphen des Alten Testaments.* Two volumes. Tübingen: Mohr, 1900.

LaCocque, A. "Date et milieu du livre de Ruth." *RHPR* 3–4 (1979): 583–93.

————. "II Zacharie." In "Aggée, Zacharie, Malachie." CAT XIC. Neuchâtel-Paris, 1981.

————. *Daniel in His Time*. Columbia, S.C.: University of South Carolina Press, 1988.

LaCocque, A. and P. *The Jonah Complex*. Atlanta: John Knox Press, 1981.

————. *Jonah, the Prophet and the Complex*. Columbia, S.C.: University of South Carolina Press, 1990.

Lévi-Strauss, C. *L'origine des manières de table*. Paris: Plon, 1968.

Levy, I. (Hebrew Text of Yerahmeel and Yosippon with a French translation and discussion). "L'histoire de 'Suzanne et les deux vieillards' dans la littérature juive." *Revue des Etudes Juives* 95 (1933): 157–66, 166–71.

Levy, L. "Die Schuhsymbolik im jüdischen Ritus." *MGWJ* 62 (1918): 182–83.

Lewy, J. "Old Assyrian puru'um and purum." *RHA* 36 (1938): 117–24.

Lipiński, E. "Le mariage de Ruth." *VT* 26 (1976): 124–27.

Lods, A. *Histoire de la littérature hébraïque et juive*. Paris: Payot, 1950.

Loretz, O. "The Theme of the Ruth Story." *CBQ* 22 (1960): 391–99.

McKane, W. "A Note on Esther IX and 1 Samuel XV." *JTS* 12 (1961): 260–61.

Meinhold, A. "Die Gattung der Josephsgeschichte und des Estherbuches: Diasporanovelle II." *ZAW* 88 (1976): 73–93.

————. *Das Buch Esther*. TVZ/AT 13. Theologischer Vlg. Zurich, 1983.

Menasce, J. de. "Daniel." In *Bible de Jérusalem*. Paris: Les Editions du Cerf, 1954.

Metzger, B. M. *An Introduction to the Apocrypha*. London and New York: Oxford University Press, 1957.

Meyers, C. L. "The Roots of Restriction: Women in Early Israel." In *The Bible and Liberation: Political and Social Hermeneutics,* edited by N. K. Gottwald. Maryknoll, N.Y.: Orbis, 1983.

———. *Discovering Eve.* New York and London: Oxford University Press, 1988.

Montefiore, C. G., and Loewe, H. *A Rabbinic Anthology.* New York: World, 1963.

Montley, P. "Judith in the Fine Arts: The Appeal of the Archetypal Androgyne." *Anima* 4 (1978): 37–42.

Moore, C. A. *Esther.* AB 7B. Garden City, N.Y.: Doubleday, 1971.

———. *Daniel, Esther, and Jeremiah: The Additions.* AB 44. Garden City, N.Y.: Doubleday, 1977.

———. *Judith.* AB 40. Garden City, N.Y.: Doubleday, 1985.

Neher, A. *The Exile of the Word: From the Silence of the Bible to the Silence of Auschwitz.* Philadelphia: Jewish Publication Society of America, 1981.

Nickelsburg, G. W. E. *Jewish Literature between the Bible and the Mishnah.* Philadelphia: Fortress Press, 1981.

Niditch, S. "Legends of Wise Heroes and Heroines." In *The Hebrew Bible and Its Modern Interpreters,* 445–64. Philadelphia: Fortress Press, and Chico: Scholars Press, 1985.

———. *Underdogs and Tricksters.* San Francisco: Harper & Row, 1987.

Orlinsky, H. M. *Essays in Biblical Culture and Biblical Translation.* New York: Ktav, 1974.

Paton, L. B. *A Critical and Exegetical Commentary on the Book of Esther.* ICC. Edinburgh: T. & T. Clark, 1908.

Pettibone-Smith, L. "Ruth." *Interpreter's Bible,* volume 2. Nashville: Abingdon Press, 1953.

Porten, B. "Megillat Ruth, mivneha . . .," *Beth Mikra,* 69/2, Jan.–Mar. 1977.

Porten, B., and Strouse, E. "A Reading of Ruth." *Commentary,* 67/2, Feb. 1979.

Preminger, A., editor. *The Hebrew Bible in Literary Criticism.* New York: Ungar, 1986.

Propp, V. *Morphology of the Folktale.* Austin: University of Texas Press, 1960.

Redfield, J. M. *Nature and Culture in the Iliad: The Tragedy of Hector.* Chicago: University of Chicago Press, 1975.

Redford, D. B. *A Study of the Biblical Story of Joseph, Genesis 37-50*. Leiden: E. J. Brill, 1970.

Ringgren, H. *Esther*. ATD 16. Göttingen: Vandenhoeck & Ruprecht, 1958.

Rosenthal, L. A. "Die Josephsgeschichte, mit den Büchern Esther und Daniel verglichen." *ZAW* 15 (1895): 278-84.

Rowley, H. H. *The Servant of the Lord and Other Essays on the Old Testament*. London: Lutterworth, 1965.

Rudolph, W. *Das Buch Ruth*. Kommentar zum Alten Testament 16/2. Leipzig, 1939.

Sandmel, S. *The Enjoyment of Scripture*. New York and London: Oxford University Press, 1972.

Sasson, J. *Ruth: A New Translation with a Philological Commentary and a Formalist-Folklorist Interpretation*. Baltimore: Johns Hopkins University, 1979.

Scholes, R., and Kellogg, R. *The Nature of Narrative*. London and New York: Oxford University Press, 1966.

van Seters, J. *Abraham in History and Tradition*. New Haven and London: Yale University Press, 1975.

Stiehl, R. "Das Buch Esther." *WZKM* 53 (1956): 4-22.

Stone, M. E., editor. *Jewish Writings of the Second Temple Period*. Philadelphia: Fortress Press, 1984.

Strouse, E. See Porten, B.

Thompson, T. and D. "Some Legal Problems in the Book of Ruth." *VT* 18/1 (1968): 79-99.

Thompson, Stith. *The Motif-Index of Folk-Literature*. Bloomington, Ind.: Indiana University Press, 1955-58.

Trible, P. "Depatriarchalizing in Biblical Interpretation." *JAAR* 41 (1973): 30-48.

―――. *God and the Rhetoric of Sexuality*. Philadelphia: Westminster Press, 1978.

Unamuno, M. de. *The Tragic Sense of Life*. New York: Dover Publications, 1954 (1912).

Ungnad, A. "Eponymen." *RLA* 2 (1938): 412-57 (see 420-48).

Vesco, J. L. "La date du livre de Ruth." *RB* 74 (1967): 235-47.

Weber, M. *The Theory of Social and Economical Organization*. New York: The Free Press, 1964.

Wilamowitz-Moellendorff, U. von. *Die griechische Literatur des Altertums.* Berlin: B. G. Teubner, 1905.

Williamson, H. G. M. *Ezra and Nehemiah.* Word Biblical Commentary, 16. Waco, Texas: Word Books, 1985.

Wurmbrand, M. "A Falasha Variant of the Story of Susanna." *Biblica* 44 (1963): 29–37.

Würthwein, E. "Esther." In *Die fünf Megilloth.* HAT 18. Tübingen: Mohr, 1968.

Zimmern, H. "Zur Frage nach dem Ursprung des Purimfestes." *ZAW* 11 (1891): 157–69.

Zlotowitz, M. *The Megillah.* New York: Mesorah, 1976.

Index of
Modern Authors

133

Index of
Subjects

Index of
Ancient Sources

New Testament

Apocrypha and Pseudepigrapha

10:7—46
15:30-35—39 n.12
15:36—69

Sirach
26:13-18—13
35:15—35 n.7

Susanna
3—30

7-8—22
12—23
23—23, 30
26—23
39—23
40—23
41—30
48—26, 30
50—30

54f—21
57—26
58f—21
60—30
62—30

Wisdom
2:8—46

JEWISH AND RABBINICAL LITERATURE

Baba Bathra
14b—115
91a, b—103 n.46

Berakhot
7b—115

Eben Shoham
————75 n.51

Genesis Rabba
50—115 n.77

Jerahmeel
————25, 26, 27

Lekah Tov [Ruth]
4.17—111 n.67

Leviticus Rabba
19—25

Megillah
————79 n.62
7a—68
16a—75

Mekhilta Exodus
————81 n.67

(Midrash) (Megillath)
  Esther (Rabba)
————66 n.37
————75 n.52
————80 n.66

Midrash Psalms
9:10—70 n.45

Midrash Tanhuma
————24 n.10

Mishna Sanhedrin
5.1—28 n.19
5.2—24 n.10

Mishna Yadayim
4.4—86 n.5
8.3—86 n.5

Mishna Yebamot
8.3—41 n.13

Pesiqta Kahana
16—89 n.14
124a—89 n.14

Pesiqta Rabbati
47b—81 n.67

Pirke Aboth
1:10(1:19)—24

Ruth Rabba
1:2—103 n.46
1:14—89 n.14
3:11—103 n.46
4:1—103 n.46
8:1—107 n.58

Ruth Zuta
53—103 n.46
55—111 n.67

Sanhedrin
20b—70

Shabbat
88a—80 n.66
41a—24 n.10
99b—82
100a—68

Tanhuma B
76a—82

Testament of Levi
6-7—36

Tosephta Yadayim
2.17—86 n.5

Yadayim
4:4—41 n.13, 86 n.5
8:3—86 n.5

Yad Hammelekh
————79 n.62

Yalkut Shimeoni
4:13—103 n.46

Yashar Wayesheb
88a-89a—27

Yebamot
63a—115 n.77
76b—41 n.13

Yosippon
10:296-98—69

Zohar
2.3a—17

ANCIENT LITERATURE